INTERNATIONAL FINANCIAL REPOATING STANDARDS
ITS WORLD-WIDE ADOPTABILITY

INTERNATIONAL FINANCIAL REPORTING STANDARDS
ITS WORLD-WIDE ADOPTABILITY

Edited by
Dr. Suman Kalyan Chaudhury
M.Com., MBA, PGDPM & IR, LLB, Ph.D.
Reader cum Placement Officer
P.G. Department of Business Administration
Berhampur University
Berhampur
(Odisha)

DISCOVERY PUBLISHING HOUSE PVT. LTD.
NEW DELHI-110 002

Published by:
Tilak Wasan

DISCOVERY PUBLISHING HOUSE PVT. LTD.
4383/4B, Ansari Road, Darya Ganj
New Delhi-110 002 (India)
Phone : +91-11-23279245, 43596064-65
Fax : +91-11-23253475
E-mail : parul.wasan@gmail.com
discoverypublishinghouse@gmail.com
web : www.discoverypublishinggroup.com

***First Edition:* 2012**

ISBN: 978-93-5056-059-4

International Financial Reporting Standards
Its Worldwide Adoptablity

Printed at:
Shree Balaji Art Press
Delhi

Preface

Financial statements are prepared and presented for both internal and external users and for statutory requirement by many entities around the world. Although such financial statements may appear similar from country to country, they apply different criteria for the recognition of items in the financial statements. Accounting bodies all over the world and the various accounting standard setting bodies are looking to eliminate the differences persisting in various countries as to the treatment in the accounts in respect of assets, liabilities, Income and expenses etc. The main purpose is to create a condition in which the financial statements of any entity can be easily read and understood by the various users of the statement residing in different parts of the world. IFRSs are the solutions to this problem. With a view to harmonize regulations, accounting standards and procedure relating to the preparation and presentation of financial statements, International Accounting Standard Board (IASB) has formulate the Global Accounting Standard called IFRSs.

International Financial Reporting Standards (IFRS) are emerging as the primary accounting language of the world. India is joining a league of 100 plus countries by announcing the convergence of Indian GAAP with IFRS with effect from April 2011. The use of IFRS in India would have significant impact on key stakeholders by presenting both benefits as well as costs. The costs of implementing IFRS should be taken up as challenges or opportunities in order to encounter them in the right spirit to ensure smooth convergence with IFRS. India can derive maximum benefit of IFRS adoption at minimum cost by learning from the experience of other countries, by building adequate pool IFRS skills, knowledge, as well as by securing the cooperation of government and other regulatory mechanisms.

There are internal and external reasons why IFRS has become a necessity. Internally, companies that operate globally often have to accommodate accounting and reporting transactions under two different sets of Accounting Rules — *first* under local GAAP to meet tax, audit and regulatory requirements of local country and, *secondly*, under a different GAAP, which is more often based on the country where its headquarters are located, for the purpose of consolidated reporting. This, in turn, leads to maintenance of multiple books, increased effort and cost and leaves room for errors. More significantly, reconciliation of the primary reporting book and secondary reporting book —which are maintained based on different sets of GAAP becomes an eternal nightmare.

There are also external reasons that are moving governments and corporate to IFRS. Today, along with free trade, Capital markets are getting integrated, leading to an increased mobility of resources and funds. A single, globally accepted accounting and reporting standards facilitates easier comparison of investment options. This aids decisions on investments, mergers and acquisitions. Adoption of IFRS will ensure that financial statements are made available on a uniform platform and will do away the need for doing adjustments to meet regional needs. Companies that benchmark against global accounting and reporting standards stand to improve transparency and quality of financial reporting. In the changing economic environment, India cannot afford to isolate itself from global accounting practices. No doubt there are huge challenges ahead—yet there are immense opportunities for Indian accounting professionals.

This book is an attempt to explain the meaning, need and importance of IFRS, its benefits as well as the cost and complexities associated in its adoption. We hope the research scholars, consultants, financial analysts, accountants, corporate; banks, academicians and also working executives will find this book more useful and rewarding.

DR. SUMAN KALYAN CHAUDHURY

Acknowledgements

Every action requires an initiator, influencer. I am initiated into writing this book, primarily, by the inspiration provided by my students and friends in the same profession. My colleagues are always standing with for support and cheering me. Therefore, I can't but gratefully acknowledge my indebtedness to all those who have extended generous assistance in the successful accomplishment of this indispensable work. It will be a serious blunder if I forget to mention some of my colleagues Prof. Niranjan Nayak, Center Head, Koustav Business School, Dr. Kirti Ranjan Swain, Associate Prof., IPSAR Business School, Cuttack, Dr. Ashok Kumar Panigrahi, Asst. Prof., RIEET School of Business, Raipur, Prof. Ashok Kumar Panda, Dean, Astha School of Management for their ardent encouragement and beacon guidance in bringing out this work.

I profusely thank my Chairman of the institute, Er. Sundhansu Kumar Dash for his rock support and continuous push that furthered my efforts seamlessly towards quick accomplishment. My heartfelt gratitude to him.

Last but not least my heartfelt gratitude to my wife Sinu knows no bounds for her immaculate co-operation. Needless to depict, I am indebted to my family members for their love and affection and inspired me in my problem solving while in action.

I am also much beholden to Mr. Tilak Wasan, Managing Director, Discovery Publishing House Pvt. Ltd. New Delhi for publishing the work in a record time.

DR. SUMAN KALYAN CHAUDHURY

Contents

Contributors

1. **Dr. Ashok Kumar Panigrahi**, Associate Professor, Department of Commerce and Management, REET School of Management, Raipur, Chhattisgarh.
2. **Dr. Arvinda. S,** Professor, Department of Management, College of Business and Economics, Adi-Haqi Campus, Mekelle University, P.O. Box: 451, Mekelle, Tigray, Ethiopia.
3. **Prof. Trilok Nath Shukla**, Sr. Lecturer, Bharatiya Vidya Bhavan, Bhubaneswar, Orissa.
4. **Dr. Suman Kalyan Chaudhury**, M.Com., MBA, PGDPM & IR, LLB, Ph.D. Reader cum Placement Officer, P.G. Department of Business Administration, Berhampur University, Berhampur(Odisha).
5. **Dr. Jagdish. R. Raiyani,** Asst. Prof., Faculty of Management, Shree Maharshi Dayanand Saraswati MBA College, Tankara, Rajkot (Gujarat).
6. **Dr. Hitesh D. Vyas**, Head, Department of Business Management, M.J. College of Commerce, Bhavanagar University, Bhavanagar, Gujurat - 364002.
7. **Mr. Suresh Kumar Sahoo**, Sr. Lecturer in Finance, REC, Bhubaneswar.
8. **Miss. Archita De**, Student, PGP-II, Bhartiya Vidya Bhavan, Bhavan's Centre for Communication and Management, Bhubaneswar, Odisha.

9. **Dr. Fisseha Girmay Tessema**, Assistant Professor, Department of Accounting and Finance, College of Business and Economics, Mekelle University, Mekelle, Ethiopia.
10. **Dr. P. Paramashivaiah,** Professor, P.G. Dept of Commerce and Management, Palace Road, Bangalore - 560 001, India
11. **Prof. Radhakrishna Mishra**, Asst. Prof. Finance, Innovation Business School, Bhubaneswar, Odisha.

International Financial Reporting Standards and Indian Corporate

Dr. Ashok Panigrahi

ABSTARCT

Globalization promotes many countries to expand their business across the borders and it also opens their doors to foreign investment. In addition to this many changes also took place like integration of international capital market; which forces business community to adopt uniform accounting standards all over the world because, different accounting frameworks in different countries leads to inconsistent accounting treatment as well as creates confusion for users of financial statements; and inconsistent accounting treatment leads to inefficiency in capital markets across the world. Adoption of IFRS is an attempt to establish a global standard for the preparation of public company financial statements in order to integrate domestic businesses with the global investor and financial community so that there is no language barrier. Its implementation is expected to result in a fusion of benefits and costs. In this regard, this article analyzes the issues, challenges, costs and benefits of migrating to IFRS with reference to India.

Keywords: Financial Statement, Accounting Standard, GAAP, ICAI.

Introduction

Financial statements are prepared and presented for both internal and external users and for statutory requirement by many entities around the world. Although such financial statements may appear similar from country to country, they apply different criteria for the recognition of items in the financial statements. With a view to harmonize regulations, accounting standards and procedure relating to the preparation and presentation of financial statements, International Accounting Standard Board (IASB) has formulate the Global Accounting Standard called IFRSs. International Financial Reporting Standards (IFRS) is the latest and hottest topic among accounting professional and business community across the globe. With the opening up of economy due to globalization and business expanding rapidly beyond geography, multiple reporting system has become time consuming, require extra efforts and skill and costly. It has also been identified as hindrance for corporate growth. The International Accounting Standard Committee (IASC) is committed to eliminate these problems by developing one set standards for reporting financial statements, *i.e.* IFRS. IFRSs issued by International Accounting Standard Board (IASB) are increasingly being recognized as global reporting standards. More than 100 countries including all European Union countries and Pakistan, Bangladesh, Sri Lanka have already adopted IFRS. Barring UK and USA, by 2011 all developed and developing economies including India will be converging to IFRS. Though US has deferred its plan to implement IFRS, a major breakthrough has been achieved in US as the Securities & Exchange Commission (SEC) has allowed Non-US companies listed in US Stock exchanges to prepare their financial statements under IFRS and have given exemption to prepare financial statements under USGAAP.

On 22 January 2010, the Ministry of Corporate Affairs (MCA) issued a press release setting out the road map for International Financial Reporting Standards (IFRS) convergence in India. The road map requires IFRS to be made applicable in a phased manner. This is an historic step that will elevate Indian entities and their finance and accounting professionals to much greater heights. The publication of the road map was eagerly awaited by those who have been saying that the convergence to IFRS in India is a matter of when and 'how' and not 'if.'

Certain Indian companies have already begun to plan the conversion to IFRS. They have found that IFRS conversion is more than an accounting change and may affect many aspects of a company outside of the finance function including information technology, group structures, direct and indirect taxes, strategic plans such as an initial public offering or an acquisition, investor relations, debt arrangements, and executive compensation. For the companies covered in Phase I (see below), there is no time to lose: listed companies having net worth greater then 1000 corers in Phase I are required to start reporting IFRS results from the first quarter of year beginning 1 April 2011. Furthermore, depending on how a company elects to present comparative information in the first year, its actual date of transition could be as early as 1 April 2010. Companies in Phase I should therefore accelerate the process of conversion to IFRS to allow them to complete the project efficiently, select meaningful accounting choices, and enhance the overall quality of their financial reporting. Companies in later phases are advised that IFRS reporting may quickly become the norm in their sector and it is better to be prepared for IFRS conversion sooner, rather than later.

What is IFRS

International Financial Reporting Standards (IFRS) are standards and interpretations adopted by the International Accounting Standards Board (IASB). They comprise:

(a) International Financial Reporting Standard;

(b) International Accounting Standards;

(c) Interpretation developed by the International Financial Reporting Interpretation Committee (IFRIC) or the former Standing Interpretation Committee (SIC).

The International Financial Reporting Standards (IFRS) is a novel way of looking at accounting. IFRS is an accounting framework that establishes recognition, measurement, presentation and disclosure requirements relating to transactions and events that are reflected in the financial statements. In simple words, it is a set of international accounting standards stating how particular types of transactions and other events should be reported in financial statements. These are generally principle based standards rather than rule based standards, its application requires exercise of judgement by the preparer and auditor in incorporating principles of accounting on the basis of the economic substance of transactions.

Why IFRS

Accounting bodies all over the world and the various accounting standard setting bodies are looking to eliminate the differences persisting in various countries asto the treatment in the accounts in respect of assets, liabilities, Income and expenses etc. The main purpose is to create a condition in which the financial statements o any entity can be easily read and understood by the various users of the statement residing in different parts of the world. IFRSs are the solutions to this problem.

The rationale behind migrating to IFRS is to provide a single set of high quality, understandable and uniform accounting standards, to improve comparability, transparency in reporting to build up investors' confidence and to seek better access to international capital market at lower cost of capital. In line with the global trend, the Institute of Chartered Accountants of India (ICAI) has declared convergence with IFRS in India with effect from April 1, 2011. Globalization of Indian GAAP will offer a blend of rewards as well as challenges. Thus, the analysis of its costs and benefits is vital to access its feasibility in order to reap maximum benefits with a minimum cost and to devise strategies to face the future challenges effectively.

Conversion to IFRS offers companies a number of important benefits. Companies that operate in a global environment and comply with foreign reporting requirements can streamline their financial reporting. This will reduce related reporting costs by developing common reporting systems and will ensure consistency in statutory reporting. Furthermore, comparison and bench marking of financial data with international competitors would be possible. Adoption of IFRS will make cross border acquisitions and joint venture possible, and also provide access to foreign capital. This is because majority of stock exchanges require financial information presented according to the IFRS. Early adoption of IFRS may offer an edge to the companies over their competitors as they can claim early adoption. This, in turn, will enhance the brand value of the company. The companies can trade their shares and securities on stock exchanges world-wide. For this, most of the stock exchanges require financial statements prepared under IFRS. Another major benefit of convergence is that the management of a company can view all the companies in a group on a common platform. This will reduce the time and efforts involved to adjust the accounts in order to comply with the requirements of the national GAAP. Business acquisition would be reflected at fair value in IFRS rather than the carrying values. This would ensure greater transparency in the financial statements. The implementation of IFRS in the corporate would require trained accountants, auditors, values and actuaries. This will boost the growth of the service sector also as India can emerge as an accounting services hub. Moreover, a single set of accounting standards world-wide would ensure that auditing firms standardize their training and quality of work is maintained globally.

Implementation of IFRS would thus ensure the following benefits:

- Same language;
- Cross border investments leading to economic growth;
- Comparability of financial statements of any two companies anywhere in the world;
- Globalization of economy and world trade;
- For multinational companies;
- Consolidation of group financial statements made easier;
- Accounting and audit functions made easier and cheaper;
- Compliance with regulatory requirements of bodies such as stock exchanges.

- Mergers and acquisitions made easier;
- Access to multinational funds;
- The job of governments and standard setters in the developing countries made easier;
- The job of tax authorities made easier;
- Time and money saved by international professional accounting firms in planning and execution of accounting and audits;
- Administrative costs of accessing the capital markets around the world reduced.

Evolution of IFRS

International Financial Reporting Standards are standards adopted by the International Accounting Standards Board (IASB), an independent accounting standard-setting body, based in London, which started its operations in 2001 for developing global accounting standards. IFRS came into limelight when the European Union decided to adopt it for all its member countries in 2005. Since then, IFRS has spread swiftly all over the world. As of now, more than 12,000 companies in almost 100 nations have implemented IFRS. In 2005, countries of the European Union, Australia, New Zealand and Russia have adopted IFRS for listed enterprises. China migrated to IFRS in 2008. Brazil is expected to move in 2010, Canada, Japan and India by 2011, Mexico in 2012. US plans to move to the pattern by 2014. It is estimated that the number of countries requiring or accepting IFRS could grow to 150 in the next few years. In India, Accounting Standards will undergo significant change from 1st April 2011, when the IFRS come into force as per the recent proposal of 1CAI which was announced in July 2007. In the first wave, IFRS. will be implemented in the Public interest entities such as listed companies, banks, insurance companies, mutual funds, financial institutions, companies with a turnover of more than one billion rupees in the preceding year, companies with a borrowing of more than 250 million rupees in the preceding year and holding or subsidiary of the above stated companies.

IFRS Compliance

As per IAS 1, an entity is said to have complied with IFRS if it has complied with

i. All IAS and IFRS

ii. All IFRIC and SICs

iii. Apply all the pronouncements of National standard setter to the extent they are consistent with other IFRS, SICs, IFRICs & IASB framework.

Advantages of Convergence/Adoption of IFRS

- Only one set of Financial Statement will be prepared under IFRS as against multiple set of financial statement as per requirement of different regulators.
- Universal financial reporting language.
- Easy comparison of Financial Statement.
- Due to preparation of only one set of financial statement under IFRS, it will be cost effective and time saving.
- Cost of raising funds from abroad will be cheaper.

Benefits to Stakeholders

Change is the order of the modern era. Changing over to IFRS fetch variety of benefits to the economy in general and to the diverse stakeholders in particular:

1. *The Investors*: Convergence with IFRS makes accounting information more reliable, relevant, timely and comparable across different legal frameworks and requirements as it would then be prepared using a common set of accounting standards thus facilitating those who want to invest outside India. Convergence with IFRS also develops better understanding of financial statements globally and also develops increased confidence among the investors.
2. *The Industry*: The other important set of beneficiary as the researchers perceive is the industry which in the event of convergence with IFRS will be benefited because of, one, increased confidence in the minds of the foreign investors,

two, decreased burden of financial reporting, three, it would simplify the process of preparing the individual and group financial statements, four, it leads to lower cost of preparing the financial statements using different sets of accounting standards.

3. *Accounting Professionals*: Although there would be initial teething problems, convergence with IFRS would definitely benefit the accounting professionals as the later would then be able to sell their expertise in various parts of the world.
4. *The Corporate World*: Convergence with IFRS would raise the reputation and relationship of the Indian corporate world with the international financial community. Moreover, the corporate houses back in India would be benefited because of ,one, achievement of higher level of consistency between the internal and external reporting, two, because of better access to international market, three, convergence with IFRS improves the risk rating and makes the corporate world more competitive globally as their comparability with the international competitors increases.
5. *The Economy*: All the discussions made above explains how convergence with IFRS would help industry grow and is advantageous to the corporate houses in the country as this would bring higher level of consistency between the internal and external reporting along with improving the risk rating among the international investors. Moreover the international comparability also improves benefiting the industrial and capital markets in the country.

Challenges in the Convergence with IFRS

Looking at the various benefits, the policy makers in India have now realized the need to follow IFRS and it is expected that a large number of Indian companies would be required to follow IFRS from 2011. There are a number of challenges that India is likely to face while dealing with convergence with IFRS. In fact convergence with IFRS is not just a technical exercise but also involves an overall change in not only the perspective but also the very objective of accounting in the country. The key areas that require close attention while dealing with conversion from Indian GAAP to IFRS are as follows:

Need For Regulatory Amendments

The success of convergence with IFRS depends on the extent to which the national GAAP, legal and regulatory issues are amended to meet the requirements of IFRS; otherwise, the conversion process may not yield fruitful results. For instance, the Companies Act (Schedule VI) prescribes the format for presentation of financial statements for Indian companies, whereas the presentation requirements are significantly different under IFRS. Thus, the Companies Act needs to be modified in line with IFRS.

Differences in Economic Environment

Every country has a unique culture, especially business culture. The economic conditions prevailing in each economy may be distinct in nature. Having a common set of international accounting standards may hinder the conveying of certain company specific information which is incomparable with others. For example, in India, even large publicly traded companies have a large number of related party transactions. Thus, there is general requirement in India to disclose related party transactions as per AS 18. But it is not extensively covered by IFRS. Another issue to be tackled is that many countries including India do not have the adequate depth and breadth for reliable determination of fair values and they oppose the use of fair value approach, whereas IFRS is very much in favor of fair valuation principles.

Lack of Readiness

IFRS conversion will involve a fundamental change to an entity's financial reporting systems, processes and effects on business performance. Hence, conversion process requires the dissemination of IFRS knowledge throughout the organization to ensure its application on an ongoing basis. But many Indian corporations are unprepared to fully adapt to IFRS because they just consider this process as an accounting issue which can be left to the finance function and auditors.

Scarcity of Resource Pool

The number of accounting professionals with adequate practical experience on convergence process is lacking. As a result, the companies will have to rely on external advisors and auditors. Besides, the accounting professionals, auditors as well as their staff need to be well-trained to function under IFRS environment. It is also important to modify the syllabus of universities, colleges, and professional accounting bodies such as ICWA, ICAI etc. to broaden the pool of trained resources.

Costly Exercise

Migrating to IFRS involves significant costs in terms of money, time and effort. There will be one-time cost of converting to IFRS including costs of internal personnel time, implementing IT systems, costs to dismantling the standard setting infrastructure and application ofrevised reporting policies, processes etc. In addition, educating all the stakeholders such as accountants, auditors, investors, regulators, employees, lenders, university faculty etc., would be a greater challenge within the prescribed time limit.

Burden For Small and Medium Enterprises (SMEs)

Though the adoption of IFRS was made mandatory for public interest entities in the first phase, if any SME wants to implement IFRS it may find it too voluminous. They may also face the barriers such as huge cost; shortage of resources, expertise, etc. Keeping in view the difficulties faced by the SMEs, the IASB is developing an IFRS for SMEs.

Conceptual Divergence

There is a common assumption that differences between Indian GAAP and IFRS are few as the former has been formulated on the basis of the principles of latter. It does not mean that the efforts required for convergence is minimum. There are significant differences between Indian GAAP and IFRS, differences in practical implementation and interpretation of similar standards in areas such as presentation of financial statements, accounting of financial instruments, business combinations etc. These differences must be harmonized to reap the real benefits of IFRS.

Impact On Financial Performance

Due to significant divergences between Indian GAAP and IFRS, the adoption of IFRS may have material impact on the financial performance of Indian organizations. The areas such as employee compensation, structuring of ESOP schemes, tax planning, and compliance with debt covenants etc. may experience substantial change. Besides, IFRS may also affect on the financial statements, loan loss provisioning, impairment charges, financial instruments and, thereby on capital adequacy ratios of financial institutions.

Suggestions

On the basis of above analysis, the following suggestions are drawn:

i. The government and other regulators like SEBI, RBI, accounting standard setting bodiess hould act in consensus to achieve high level of integration with IFRS without any bias;

ii. SMEs should be enabled to adopt simplified version of IFRS so that the financial statements of all entities irrespective of listed/unlisted, public/private and large/small can be synchronized across national borders;

iii. The curriculum of universities and other professional accounting bodies should be reformulated to include IFRS principles and adequate training should be provided to faculty members to facilitate them in teaching.

Applicability of IFRS In India

IFRS will be implemented in India in three different phases:

Phase I: Effective from 1st April 2011

i. Sensex 30 Companies

ii. Nifty 50 Companies

iii. Listed and Non-listed Companies having Net Worth of more than Rs.1000 Crore as on 1st April 2009.

Phase II: Effective from 1st April 2012

i. Listed and Non-listed companies with net worth of more than Rs. 500 Crores;

ii. Insurance Companies.

Phase III: Effective from 1st April 2013

i. All listed Companies with Net worth of less than Rs.500 Crore

ii. Banking Companies.

Conclusion

International Financial Reporting Standards (IFRS) are emerging as the primary accounting language of the world. India is joining a league of 100 plus countries by announcing the convergence of Indian GAAP with IFRS with effect from April 2011. The use of IFRS in India would have significant impact on key stakeholders by presenting both benefits as well as costs. The costs of implementing IFRS should be taken up as challenges or opportunities in order to encounter them in the right spirit to ensure smooth convergence with IFRS. India can derive maximum benefit of IFRS adoption at minimum cost by learning from the experience of other countries, by building adequate pool IFRS skills, knowledge, as well as by securing the cooperation of government and other regulatory mechanisms.

In the changing economic environment, India cannot afford to isolate itself from global accounting practices. Not shout it. Irrespective of changes required in our legislation and resources needed for convergence to IFRS, sooner the better for economic prosperity. There are huge challenges ahead—yet there are immense opportunities for Indian accounting professionals.

REFERENCES

1. Anuradha H.N. "IFRS in India — Benefits *Vs.* Costs", *The Management Accountant,* August 2010, (659-661).
2. Mishra S.K. "IFRS — The New Era of Accounting", *The Management Accountant,* August 2010, (668-679).
3. Indapurkar Kavita, Chakraborty Anindita, Pathak Ravindra, "Convergence with IFRS : Hopes and Challenges" , www.indianmba.com

4. http://www.taxguru.in/accounting/ministry-of-corporate-affairs-issues-roadmap-for-ifrs-conversion-in-india.html

5. Lantto, Anna-Maija and Sahlström, Petri (2009), Impact of International Financial Reporting Standard Adoption on Key Financial Ratios, *Accounting and Finance*, 49, 341–361.

6. Armstrong, Chris S., Barth, Mary E., Jagolinzer, Alan D. and Riedl, Edward J. (2009). Market Reaction to the Adoption of IFRS in Europe, *Accounting Review Forthcoming.*

7. Ball, Ray (2005). International Financial Reporting Standards (IFRS): Pros and Cons for Investors, *Accounting and Business Research, Forthcoming.*

8. Daske, Holger, Hail, Luzi, Leuz, Christian and Verdi, Rodrigo S. (2008), Mandatory IFRS Reporting Around the World: Early Evidence on the Economic Consequences, ECGI — *Finance Working Paper No. 198/2008; Chicago GSB Research Paper No. 12.*

9. De Jong, Abe, Rosellón Cifuentes, Miguel Angel and Verwijmeren, Patrick (2006), The Economic Consequences of IFRS: The Impact of IAS 32 on Preference Shares in the Netherlands, *ERIM Report Series* Reference No. ERS-2006-021-F&A.

10. Hboxma (2008), Economics and IFRS, Retrieved on October 14, 2009 from http://www.oppapers.com/essays/Economics-Ifrs/177415.

11. Callao, Susana, Ferrer, Cristina, Jarne, Jose I. and Lainez, Jose A. (2009), The impact of IFRS on the European Union: Is It Related to the Accounting Tradition of the Countries? *Journal of Applied Accounting Research,* 10(1), 33 – 55.

12. Carmona, Salvador and Trombetta, Marco (2008), On the Global Acceptance of IAS/IFRS Accounting Standards: The Logic and Implications of the Principles-based System, *Journal of Accounting and Public Policy,* 27(6).

13. Ramanna, Karthik and Sletten, Ewa (2009), Why Do Countries Adopt International Financial Reporting Standards? *Harvard Business School Accounting & Management Unit Working Paper No. 09-102.*

14. P. Vandana Saxena, CEO, Get Through Guides, "IFRS IMPLEMENTATION AND CHALLENGES IN INDIA", Published in *MEDC Monthly Economic Digest,* Aug. 2009.

International Financial Reporting Standards
Hopes and Challenges

Jagdish. R. Raiyani

ABSTRACT

International Financial Reporting Standards (IFRS) adopted by International Accounting Standards Board (IASB) is a standardized format of financial reporting that is gaining momentum world-wide and is a single consistent accounting framework and is likely to become predominant GAAP in times to come. In this world of globalization in which Indian economy has also flourished, adopting IFRS would not only make Indian companies at par with other global companies but shall also increase India's marketability globally in terms of foreign investments. The Chapter makes an attempt to understand the various beneficiaries by adopting IFRS, the challenges faced by India in adopting the same and the likely risks in introducing IFRS. The chapter also makes an attempt to analyze the requirements for successful implementation of IFRS in India.

Conceptual Framework

International Financial Accounting Standards (IFRS), formerly known as International Accounting Standards (IAS) are the Standards, Interpretations and Framework for the Preparation and Presentation of Financial Statements adopted by the International Accounting Standards Board (IASB). IAS was issued in 1973 and 2001 by the board of the Internal Accounting Standards Committee (IASC). On April 1, 2001 the new IASB took over the responsibility of setting International Accounting Standards from IASC. It has since then continued to develop standards called as the new standards IFRS.

Structure of IFRS

IFRS are as principles based set of standards that establish broad rules and also dictate specific treatments. International Financial Reporting Standards comprises of:

- International Financial Reporting Standards (IFRS)-standards issued after 2001;
- International Accounting Standards (IAS) — standards issued before 2001;
- Interpretations originated from the International Financial Reporting Interpretations Committee (IFRIC) — issued after 2001;
- Standing Interpretations Committee (SIC) — issued before 2001.

Framework for the Preparation and Presentation of Financial Statements

There is also a Framework for the Preparation and Presentation of Financial Statements which describes of the principles underlying IFRS. A framework is nothing but the foundation of accounting standards. The framework states that the objectives of financial statements is to provide information about the financial position, performance and changes in the financial position of an entity that is useful to a wide range of users in making economic decisions, and to provide the current financial status of the entity to its shareholders and public in general.

IFRS financial statements consist of (IAS1.8)

- Statement of Financial Position.
- Comprehensive income statement.
- Statement of changes in equity (SOCE) or a statement of recognized income or expense ("SORIE").
- Cash flow statement or statement of cash flows.
- Notes (including summary of the significant accounting policies).

Meaning of Convergence with IFRS

Convergence with IFRS implies to achieve harmony with IFRSs and to design and maintain national accounting standards in a way that they comply with the International Accounting Standards. The transition would enable Indian entities to be fully IFRS compliant and give an "unreserved and explicit statement of compliance with IFRS" in their financial statements.

In the new format core accounting principles will still apply and simply is an additional piece of accounting equation. The new IFRS are nothing but the new International Accounting Rules.

Many of the standards forming part of IFRS are known by the older name of International Accounting Standards (IAS). IAS was issued between 1973 and 2001 by the Board of the International Accounting Standards Committee (IASC). On 1 April 2001, the new IASB took over the responsibility for setting International Accounting Standards from the IASC. During its first meeting the new Board adopted existing IAS and SICs. The IASB has continued to develop standards calling the new standards IFRS. It is simply an addition to the existing accounting rules.

Review of Literature

De Jong, Rosellón Cifuentes, and Verwijmeren (2006) demonstrated one of the economic implications of international standards. The study revealed that 71 per cent of the firms that are affected by IAS buy back their preference shares or alter the specifications of the preference shares in such a way that the classification as equity can be maintained. The paper concluded that IFRS does not only lead to a decrease in the use of financial instruments that otherwise would have added to the capital structure diversity, but also changes firm's real capital structure.

Hboxma (2008) pointed out that the most significant discrepancy between the two sets of standards in accounting treatment of business combination, provisions financial instruments and business assets with reference to both net income and share holder's equity while the individual accounting differences in property, plant and equipment show a significant difference only on share holders' equity.

Daske *et al.* (2008) asserted that on average, market liquidity increases around the time of the introduction of IFRS. A decrease in firms' cost of capital and an increase in equity valuations was also observed, but only if it is accounted for the possibility that the effects occur prior to the official adoption date. On partitioning of sample, the researchers found that the capital-market benefits occur only in countries where firms have incentives to be transparent and where legal enforcement is strong.

Callao *et al.* (2009) found that first application of IFRS has had different effects on the financial reporting among countries. The cluster analysis identifies four groups which show that the impact of IFRS on financial statements of European firms is not related to traditional accounting systems.

Carmona and Trombetta (2008) evaluated the logic and implications of the principles-based system and suggested that the principles-based approach to the standards and its inner flexibility enables the application of IAS/IFRS to countries with diverse accounting traditions and varying institutional conditions. Furthermore, he said that "the principles-based approach involves major changes in the expertise held by accountants and, hence, in their educational background, training programmes and in the organizational and business models of accounting firms".

Ramanna and Sletten (2009) studied a sample of 102 non-European Union countries and found the variations in the decision to adopt International Financial Reporting Standards (IFRS) and revealed that more powerful countries are less likely to adopt IFRS, consistent with more powerful countries being less willing to surrender standard-setting authority to an international body. They also find no evidence that levels of and expected changes in foreign trade and investment flows in a country whether affect its adoption decision. Thus, it cannot be confirmed that IFRS lowers information costs in more globalized economies. They further concluded that a country likely to adopt IFRS if its trade partners or countries within in its geographical region are IFRS adopters.

Lantto and Sahlström (2009) studied the impact of International Financial Reporting Standard adoption on key financial ratios and revealed increase profitability ratios and decrease in price to earnings ratio; decrease in liquidity ratio; increase in gearing ratio and decrease in equity ratios. The results of the study indicated that the adoption of IFRS changes the magnitudes of the key accounting ratios of Finnish companies by considerably increasing the profitability ratios and gearing ratio moderately, and considerably decreasing the PE ratio and equity and quick ratios slightly.

Armstrong *et al.* (2009) examined European stock market reactions to 16 events associated with the adoption of International Financial Reporting Standards (IFRS) in Europe and found an incrementally positive reaction for firms with lower quality pre-adoption information, which is more pronounced in banks, and with higher pre-adoption information asymmetry, consistent with investors expecting net information quality benefits from IFRS adoption. They finally concluded a positive reaction to IFRS adoption events for firms with high quality pre-adoption information, consistent with investors expecting net convergence benefits from IFRS adoption.

Ball (2005) showed concern about substantial differences among the countries' implementation of IFRS, which may have risk uniformity. The researcher also feels that simply having uniform standards may not produce the required impact of uniform financial reporting if the approach and objectives of accounting differ.

Objectives of the Study

The present conceptual paper has been prepared keeping in view the following objectives:

- To develop an insight about the global financial reporting language *i.e.* IFRS;
- To know about the likely beneficiaries of convergence of Indian GAAP with IFRS;
- To study the challenges and risks specific to India in adoption of IFRS;
- To give suggestions towards successful implementation of IFRS.

Discussion of the Objectives

Beneficiaries of Convergence with IFRS

The researchers point out several beneficiaries to the convergence of Indian GAAP with IFRS. Some important ones are discussed as below.

1. *The Investors:* Convergence with IFRS makes accounting information more reliable, relevant, timely and comparable across different legal frameworks and requirements as it would then be prepared using a common set of accounting standards thus facilitating those who want to invest outside India. Convergence with IFRS also develops better understanding of financial statements globally and also develops increased confidence among the investors.
2. *The Industry:* The other important set of beneficiary as the researchers perceive is the industry which in the event of convergence with IFRS will be benefited because of, one, increased confidence in the minds of the foreign investors, two, decreased burden of financial reporting, three, it would simplify the process of preparing the individual and group financial statements, four, it leads to lower cost of preparing the financial statements using different sets of accounting standards.
3. *Accounting Professionals:* Although there would be initial teething problems, convergence with IFRS would definitely benefit the accounting professionals as the later would then be able to sell their expertise in various parts of the world.
4. *The Corporate World:* Convergence with IFRS would raise the reputation and relationship of the Indian corporate world with the international financial community. Moreover, the corporate houses back in India would be benefited because of, one, achievement of higher level of consistency between the internal and external reporting, two, because of better access to international market, three, convergence with IFRS improves the risk rating and makes the corporate world more competitive globally as their comparability with the international competitors increases.

5. *The Economy:* All the discussions made above explains how convergence with IFRS would help industry grow and is advantageous to the corporate houses in the country as this would bring higher level of consistency between the internal and external reporting along with improving the risk rating among the international investors. Moreover the international comparability also improves benefiting the industrial and capital markets in the country.

Challenges in the Convergence with IFRS Faced by India

Looking at the various benefits, the policy makers in India have now realized the need to follow IFRS and it is expected that a large number of Indian companies would be required to follow IFRS from 2011. There are a number of challenges that India is likely to face while dealing with convergence with IFRS. In fact convergence with IFRS is not just a technical exercise but also involves an overall change in not only the perspective but also the very objective of accounting in the country. The researcher points out certain key areas that require close attention while dealing with conversion from Indian GAAP to IFRS.

It has to be realized that this conversion is not just the any technical exercise. Even after the later gets introduced, the preparers, users and auditors will continue to encounter practical implementation challenges. This is because the consequences of the same would have far wider financial reporting issues and extend to various significant business and regulatory matters like, structuring of ESOP schemes, training of employees, tax planning, modification of IT system, compliance with debt covenants and so on. Another important challenge is to ensure that their investors understand the shift from Indian GAAP to IFRS.

It is a common belief that there are only a few differences between Indian GAAP and IFRS as the former is inspired by the later. Although it is true but this does not mean that the efforts required for conversion would get minimal. This is because the areas where the differences lie are deep routed for example, fixed assets accounting, presentation of financial statements, accounting of financial instruments and foreign exchange, group accounts etc. Indian GAAP is still a long way behind IFRS..

Moreover in spite of any number of arguments in favor of convergence with IFRS deviations are bound to exist due to various conceptual, practical, legal and implementation challenges that cause unavoidable reasons for departures from IFRS.

The first and foremost challenge is that of maintaining consistency with the legal and the regulatory requirements prevalent in India. For example, Accounting Standard (AS) 25 (Interim financial Reporting), does not require disclosure and presentation of interim financial statements in India because here at present Clause 41 of the Listing Agreement prescribes a format of presentation of quarterly and/or half yearly financial results and also requires various disclosure to be made therein. Similarly, (AS) 21 defines 'control' as ownership of more than half of the voting power of an enterprise or control over the composition of the governing body of an enterprise. This definition of control is based on definitions of holding company and subsidiary company as per Companies Act 1956. However, IAS 27 defines control as "the power to govern the financial and operating policies of an enterprise so as to obtain benefits from its activities".

Another important reason for departure from IFRS may be the macro environment of the country where it is applied. For example in view of the fact that various markets in the country are not supposed to possess the necessary depth and breadth , there has been reluctance in India to adopt FAIR VALUE approach in measurement of various assets and liabilities where as IFRS is based on the fair value approach.

It is predicted by the think tanks of the country that a sudden convergence with IFRS may cause hardships to the Indian industry. The industry therefore requires to be prepared for adoption of IFRS for which modifications are required to be made in the Accounting Standards. For example the revised version of AS 15 permits deferment of expenditure incurred on account of termination of services arising in a voluntary retirement scheme for transitional period in view of the fact that the Indian industry was undergoing structural changes at the time when this standard was introduced. As against this, IAS 19 does not allow the deferment of such expenditure even as a transitional measure.

The conceptual differences are also likely exist that may cause departure from IFRS. For example AS 29 does not specifically deal with constructive obligation whereas IAS 37 deals specifically with this in the context of creation of a provision. The effect of this is that in some cases provisions will be required to be recognized at an early stage.

Everybody is reluctant to change and this is a universal fact. Unhelpful attitude of corporate world poses another challenge in convergence with IFRS standards.

Similarly implementation challenges also crop in the convergence with IFRS because of complexities of the recognition and measurement requirements and the extent of disclosures required by IFRS on different types of entities that are public interest and other than public interest entities. Again the criteria regarding which entities should be considered as public interest entities for the purpose of application of IFRS may prove to be another critical issue that may pose implementation problems. These and other such issues pose challenges in convergence with IFRS. A movement was initiated by an International body called 'International Organization of Securities Commissions (IOSCO) to harmonize diverse disclosure practices followed in different countries.

There are significant differences between IFRS and Indian-GAAP. In fact, Indian Accounting Standards have not kept pace with changes in IFRS. This is because Indian Standards remain sensitive to local conditions, including the legal and economic environment.

Risks Involved in Introducing IFRS in India

- The researchers feel that the biggest risk in converging Indian GAAP with IFRS is the fact that the accounting entities underestimate the complexity involved in the process. Instead it should be recognized well in advance that teething problems would definitely creep in. Converting to IFRS will increase the complexity with the introduction of concepts such as present value and fair value. Similarly there are some recognition and measurement issues that would create quite a lot of controversy.

- Implementing IFRS has increased financial reporting risk due to technical complexities, manual work arounds and management time taken up with implementation.
- Another risk involved is that the IFRS do not recognize the adjustments that are prescribed through court schemes and consequently all such items will be recorded through income statement.
- In IFRS framework, treatment of expenses like premium payable on redemption of debentures, discount allowed on issue of debentures, underwriting commission paid on issue of debentures etc is different than the present method used. This would bring about a change in income statement leading to enormous confusion and complexities.
- IFRS will introduce changes in the very concepts and definitions of in a few areas like change in the definition of 'equity'. This would result in tax benefits of hybrid instruments where 'interest' is treated as receiving a dividend.
- At the ground level, it will be difficult for the small firms and the accounting companies to keep pace with the process of convergence with IFRS and it will be more challenging for them. Basically the idea is that it should be made mandatory for the companies to prepare consolidated financial statements which would require them to provide information about their unlisted companies as well under IFRS. This may however result in increased challenges to the small and medium firms in the country.
- IFRS financial statements are significantly more complex than financial statements based on Indian GAAP. This complexity threatens to undermine the usefulness of IFRS financial statements in making decisions. The risk is that the preparation of financial reports will become just a technical compliance exercise rather than a mechanism for communicating performance and the financial position of companies.
- Laws and pronouncements are always country specific and no country can abandon its own laws altogether. It will always

be checked to see if the IFRS pronouncements fit for application in a particular country and its environment.

In fact it is not yet very clear whether IFRS would be directly adopted or will they converge into Indian GAAP. This also shows our unpreparedness towards the convergence process.

Successful Implementation

Looking at the risks we cannot escape or avoid from converging or accepting IFRS. There is a strong case for convergence and harmonizing accounting principles and standards at the international level. This goes more strongly with India as we have witnessed a good growth with globalization and it has helped Indian companies to raise funds from offshore capital market. Therefore, the researchers feel that instead of adopting an escapist path India should go along and face the challenges, study the likely risks and accordingly get prepared for IFRS. The researchers point out some suggestions for successful implementation of IFRS.

If India does not have an active role in standard setting process internationally, converging to IFRS using an endorsement process and possibly accepting temporary carve outs and quirks seems to be a safer route to take. In view of various challenges and difficulties it seems to be more appropriate to adopt all IFRSs from a specified future date as it is. This method has been successfully adopted by many countries. ICAI has also decided to adopt IFRS for public interest entities from accounting periods commencing on or after April 2011.

Tax authorities should consider IFRS implications on direct and indirect taxes and provide appropriate guidance from a tax perspective. The Institute of Chartered Accountants of India should make an all out effort to train and upgrade the profession in IFRS.

Successful implementation of IFRS would require companies to fully use IFRS as their basis of daily primary financial reporting as well as for performance tracking in the form of budgets, forecast and management accounts. IFRS requires industry specialization. But due to lack of industry specific guidance in

IFRS and general reliance on Indian GAAP there are no industry specific themes in IFRS. Implementation in other countries has not revealed any visible pattern in industry wise adoption of these standards. There is need to improve upon the disclosures which may help to view financial statements not only from compliance perspective but also as a way of communicating and explaining performance.

It should be made compulsory for the companies to prepare IFRS compliant statements along with Indian GAAP compliant statements so that the likely problems can be traced in advance and corrected as far as possible.

Thus to implement IFRS successfully and smoothly, a high degree of mutual international understanding about corporate objectives, financial reporting objectives and harmonization objectives need to be achieved.

Suggestions for Increased Convergence

The researchers put forward certain suggestions to enable harmonization in published company annual reports at the international level.

i. Political pressure on International Accounting Standards Board (IASB) should be avoided from various interest groups like private sector and government agencies.

ii. IASB should publicize standards developed by it and get support from the accounting profession, member countries and corporate management all over the world.

iii. IASB should encourage member bodies to adopt IFRS and formulate and reformulate their rules that they are in line with IFRS.

iv. Legislation should be passed to the effect that in case of any changes or amendments in IASB, the local standards, if any, should be brought in line with these.

v. Local stock exchange can be used for cooperating in taking action against companies that fail to comply with the IFRS.

vi. Governing bodies of the various accounting profession can also be used to apply disciplinary procedures in case of nan-convergence with IFRS.

Conclusion

Looking at the present scenario of the world economy and the position of India convergence with IFRS can be strongly recommended. But at the same time it can also be said that this transition to IFRS will not be a swift and painless process. Implementing IFRS would rather require change in formats of accounts, change in different accounting policies and more extensive disclosure requirements. Therefore all parties concerned with financial reporting also need to share the responsibility of international harmonization and convergence. Keeping in mind the fact that IFRS is more a principle based approach with limited implementation and application guidance and moves away from prescribing specific accounting treatment all accountants whether practicing or non-practicing have to participate and contribute effectively to the convergence process. This would lead to subsequent revisions from time to time arising from its global implementation and would help in formulation of future international accounting standards. A continuous research is in fact needed to harmonize and converge with the international standards and this in fact can be achieved only through mutual international understanding both of corporate objectives and rankings attached to it.

REFERENCES

1. Lantto, Anna-Maija and Sahlström, Petri (2009). Impact of International Financial Reporting Standard Adoption on Key Financial Ratios, *Accounting and Finance*, 49, 341–361.
2. Armstrong, Chris S., Barth, Mary E., Jagolinzer, Alan D. and Riedl, Edward J. (2009), Market Reaction to the Adoption of IFRS in Europe, *Accounting Review Forthcoming.*
3. Ball, Ray (2005), International Financial Reporting Standards (IFRS): Pros and Cons for Investors, *Accounting and Business Research, Forthcoming.*
4. Daske, Holger, Hail, Luzi, Leuz, Christian and Verdi, Rodrigo S. (2008), Mandatory IFRS Reporting Around the World: Early Evidence on the Economic Consequences. ECGI — *Finance Working Paper No. 198/2008; Chicago GSB Research Paper No. 12.*

5. De Jong, Abe, Rosellón Cifuentes, Miguel Angel and Verwijmeren, Patrick (2006). The Economic Consequences of IFRS: The Impact of IAS 32 on Preference Shares in the Netherlands, *ERIM Report Series* Reference No. ERS-2006-021-F&A.

6. Hboxma (2008). Economics and IFRS. Retrieved on October 14, 2009 from http://www.oppapers.com/essays/Economics-Ifrs/177415.

7. Callao, Susana, Ferrer, Cristina, Jarne, Jose I. and Lainez, Jose A. (2009), The Impact of IFRS on the European Union: Is It Related to the Accounting Tradition of the Countries? *Journal of Applied Accounting Research*, 10(1), 33-55.

8. Carmona, Salvador and Trombetta, Marco (2008), On the Global Acceptance of IAS/IFRS Accounting Standards: The Logic and Implications of the Principles-Based System, *Journal of Accounting and Public Policy*, 27(6).

International Financial Reporting Standards in Indian Context

Dr. Hitesh D. Vyas

ABSTRACT

The objective of the chapter is to examine the international financial reporting standards and to identify its implications in Indian context. The international financial reporting standards were set up in context of the objective of fair presentation can mean that additional disclosures in excess of those mandated by IFRS are necessary. The International accounting guidance exists in the IASB's framework, IFRS and Interpretations. The Framework is used as a guide by both international and national standard setters to set consistent and logical accounting standards. The Framework also assists preparers and auditors in interpreting standards and dealing with issues that the standards do not cover.

Introduction

Accounting is a one of the key function of any profitable or non-profitable activity, and standardization of the accounting is a need of the time. Different countries have different accounting standards; which reflects in their style of treatment to financial statements. Thus, the nine world-wide professional accountancy bodies were agreed to set the International Accounting Standards Committee (IASC) in 1973, The IASC renamed as International Accounting Standards Boards (IAS) in may 2000[1]. The IASB's objectives were set out in a revised constitution. The ultimate goal is the development and rigorous application of a single set of global accounting standards, which will produce high-quality financial information to help participants in the world's capital markets to make economic decisions.[2]

The Framework for Standard Setting

Framework for international standard setting involves several dedicated bodies, as well as the co-operation and input from standard setting bodies throughout the world. Nineteen Trustees have the power to appoint the members of the Standards Advisory Council (SAC), the International Accounting Standards Board (Board) and the International Financial Reporting Interpretations Committee (IFRIC). The Trustees also monitor the IASB's effectiveness, raise funds, approve the IASB's budget and take responsibility for constitutional changes.[3]

The objective of the study is to examine the international financial reporting standards and to identify its implications in Indian context. The international financial reporting standards were set up in context of the objective of fair presentation can mean that additional disclosures in excess of those mandated by IFRS are necessary. The International accounting guidance exists in the IASB's framework, IFRS and Interpretations. The Framework is used as a guide by both international and national standard setters to set consistent and logical accounting standards. The Framework also assists preparers and auditors in interpreting standards and dealing with issues that the standards do not cover.

Literature Review

The paper GAAS and the generally accepted government auditing standards — GAGAS (2008)[4] discusses the different methods of accounting that are being adopted to be used in both the public as well as private sectors. It particularly focuses on generally accepted auditing standards — GAAS and the generally accepted government auditing standards—GAGAS. The paper discusses each method and compares their use in private and public sectors. "Since the yellow book as well as the SAS No. 63 includes the function as well as reporting levels of the GAAS, the defining terms of reportable circumstances as well as material defects carry towards internal governmental regulation structural reports. The bearable limit in case of a situation of reporting is less compared to material form of weakness, even though a material form of weakness is a kind of situation of reporting. Nevertheless the dichotomy among a material form of weakness and other situations of reporting sometimes would be intricate to find out. The accounting system estimates the funds owed by the clients for usage of computer and assignments completed on task and contract orders, accounts receivable that are unbilled and income received.

An assessment of the barriers and challenges to the institution of the International Accounting Standards Board's (IASB's) international financial reporting standards (IFRS) (2008)[5] focuses on the International Accounting Standard Board's (IASB's) international financial reporting standards (IFRS) and the barriers and challenges that exist to adoption and implementation of these standards. The work conducts an extensive review of relevant academic and professional literature to identify these challenges and barriers and identifies the steps that are necessary to overcome these challenges.

In a recent report Allen Blewitt, Chief Executive of the Association of Chartered Certified Accountants (ACCA) warned that "implementation of, and compliance with, International Financial Reporting Standards would be adversely impacted unless the standards were made less complex." Blewitt specifically stated while speaking at a conference in London that: "What I believe the IASB most urgently needs to address are the barriers to implementation. From talking to our members working in business around the world, it is clear that the length of the standards and complexity of the concepts represent a very real problem in many countries. The standards have been described to me as a major turn-off and disincentive for accountants in commerce and industry."

A study of John Goodwin, Kamran Ahmed (2006). The impact of international financial reporting standards: does size matter? Managerial Auditing Journal, Vol. 21, Issue: 5, Page: 460 - 475[6] seeks to examine the impact of Australian equivalents to international financial reporting standards (A-IFRS) on the accounts of small—, medium— and large-sized firms. Design/ methodology/approach — For 135 listed Australian entities, the half-yearly accounts ended 30 June 2005 are examined to identify the effects of A-IFRS. Data are gathered on the change in major balance sheet and income statement elements, the major econciling items and earnings variability. Findings show that more than half of small firms have no change in net income or equity from A-IFRS, and that there is an increase in the number of adjustments to net income and equity with firm size. The study also finds that A-IFRS has increased net income for small- and medium-sized firms. Equity has increased (decreased) under A-IFRS for small (large) firms. Small firms experience higher earnings variability than medium-sized or large firms under A-IFRS. Research limitations/implications – The sample is limited to 31 December reporting date firms and not all A-IFRS must be complied with when firms restate their comparatives. Practical implications – Analysts, auditors and other account users should be aware that the effects of A-IFRS are correlated with firm size. Originality /value — This is the first Australian empirical paper on the effects of A-IFRS. It raises doubts about the contentions of some that A-IFRS will have widespread adverse effects on firms' accounts.

Luzi Hail (2007) Do International Financial Reporting Standards Live Up to Their Promise? November 28, 2007, Knowledge@Wharton[7] indicates that at a time when many barriers to global trade have fallen and the world's economies have become increasingly linked, countries all over the world are taking steps to harmonize their accounting standards and develop a truly global language of business. Under the lead of the International Accounting Standards Board (IASB), already more than 100 countries, most notably the European Union and many Asian economies, have either implemented International Financial Reporting Standards (IFRS) or plan to do so. So far, the United States has been a holdout. But the winds are changing. On November 15, 2007, the U.S. Securities and Exchange Commission (SEC) — which up to then was requiring foreign companies to either report using Generally

Accepted Accounting Principles (GAAP) or to reconcile to them — announced that it would promote international compatibility by allowing foreign companies to access U.S. capital markets while reporting under IFRS. At the same time, the SEC is contemplating changes that would grant domestic firms the choice between reporting under GAAP or IFRS. Proponents of accounting harmonization, and there are many, say that IFRS will enhance the comparability of financial statements, improve corporate transparency, increase the quality of financial reporting and, therefore, ultimately benefit firms and investors.

Luzi Hail and Holger Daske (2007) Mandatory IFRS Reporting Around the World: Early Evidence on the Economic Consequences University of Mannheim, Christian Leuz from the University of Chicago and Rodrigo Verdi MIT[8] studied "The issue of convergence represents a kind of revolution," the authors note. "Just a few years ago, most observers would have said there was no chance of converging U.S. accounting rules and IFRS into a single, globally accepted standard. But now it looks like it may actually happen."

The paper notes that on average, market liquidity and firm value do increase by about 2 per cent to 6 per cent for firms that adopt IFRS reporting when it becomes mandatory at least when compared to the level prior to IFRS adoption or to firms that have not yet switched. Further, total trading costs and the gap between bid and ask prices both generally decline. "In contrast to the liquidity benefits, the costs of capital results are less clear-cut," he adds. "It is possible, however, that the weaker cost of capital effects reflects temporary difficulties of forecasting earnings under the new accounting regime." Yet another possible explanation is that markets reacted earlier, before firms had in fact changed their reporting systems.

Navin Agrawal (2009), Getting IFRS right the first time, Accounting Nuances, Ernst & Young India Pvt. Ltd.[9], When companies prepare their first financial statements compliant with the International Financial Reporting Standard (IFRS), they will have to use IFRS-1—First-time Adoption of International Financial Reporting Standards. IFRS-1 prescribes procedures that a company has to follow while preparing its opening IFRS balance sheet at the beginning of the so-called comparative (comparing with the previous corresponding period) period. Thus, Indian companies preparing IFRS financial statements for the period beginning 1 April 2011 with one year comparatives would need to prepare the opening IFRS balance sheet as on 1 April 2010.

With regard to PPE, the relevant IFRS provision recognizes that entities may find it difficult to apply component approach under the accounting principle on "Property, Plant and Equipment" retrospectively. This provision provides an option to fair value various components of PPE at the date of transition to IFRS. These values will become deemed cost for subsequent applications of the relevant accounting principle.

On the four mandatory exceptions, IFRS-1 prohibits retrospective derecognition of financial assets and financial liabilities, use of hedge accounting, change of estimates and for assets classified as held for sale or discontinued operations. Regarding estimates, IFRS-1 does not allow the use of hindsight to change previous estimates. Other prohibitions on retrospective application aim at avoiding the use of hindsight as well.

A company also must apply IFRS-1 in any interim period report prepared within its first financial reporting period. As a result, companies must be capable of generating a comparative IFRS profit and loss account not only for the full year, but also for the quarters.

Lastly, IFRS-1 also requires certain disclosures to be made in the financial statements—namely, reconciliation of its equity reported under previous GAAP to its equity under IFRS as on the date of transition and at the end of the latest period presented under previous GAAP as well as reconciliation of the profit or loss reported under previous GAAP to its profit or loss under IFRS for the latest period. These disclosures will enable investors and users of financial statements to better understand the impact of convergence with IFRS.

As this overview has shown, in order to make informed decisions regarding voluntary exemptions, Indian companies will need to assess a variety of factors, including the cost of retrospective application, the availability of required information and the conversion selections made by peer companies.

International Financial Regulation: the quiet revolution, C.D. Deshmukh Memorial Lectures, Reserve Bank of India, describes that perhaps the best place to start is with the markets themselves. Why has normal market mechanisms not operated properly to weed out poorly performing institutions and create a healthy competitive financial system? There are a number of potential answers to that question. But factors which can encourage banks and other financial institutions to take on too much risk, with the occasional panic when reality takes hold, include:

So it is important to ensure, for regulators to do their job effectively, that the appropriate pre-conditions for effective banking supervision are in place. The Basel Committee defined five pre-conditions for effective supervision in banking, and I am sure that something very similar applies in the case of both investment and insurance business. They are:

An Unequal Sharing of IFRS Benefits

Overall, based on the favourable market reactions, it would appear that IFRS delivers what standard setters, firms and investors hoped for.

A closer look, however, reveals a subtler picture. "Why is it that some publicly listed companies choose to voluntarily adopt International Financial Reporting Standards early on, while others wait until it is mandated?" Hail asks. "Our results show that the greatest positive effects on firm value and liquidity appear to accrue to these early adopters. This makes perfect sense, because for them the benefits of switching to IFRS should outweigh the costs; otherwise they would not have done it."

The same reasoning helps explain why some firms hold off on implementing IFRS until they are forced to adopt the standards. "If there were no gains for these firms to adopt IFRS beforehand," he says, "why should the cost-benefit trade off all of a sudden change when they are left without choice? Obviously, there must exist some other benefits in the form of increased comparability, better risk-sharing among investors or the like that would not have occurred in the absence of the mandate."

Consequences of IFRS Reporting for U.S. Firms

The study also raises questions about the anticipated benefits of allowing U.S. firms to use IFRS in their domestic reporting. "Our findings indicate that the liquidity effects for first-time mandatory adopters are smaller in countries that have fewer differences between local GAAP and IFRS or for countries that, over several years, have been gradually converging towards IFRS reporting," says Hail. "This is consistent with the notion that, in these cases, the regulatory change is likely to be of smaller magnitude."

Regarding the U.S., with its already strong enforcement institutions and lively capital markets, Hail expects that allowing a switch to IFRS will likely cause little capital-market benefits. "The infrastructure is already in place, and combined with the strong reporting incentives due to constant pressure from investors, we may not see much of an impact on how U.S. firms report," he adds. "But perhaps U.S. firms will gain from comparability benefits, which should be more pronounced when you are late in the game and everybody else has already switched to IFRS."

Implications to Indian Context

But my own analysis suggests that, below the parapet, so to speak, there are more important and far reaching changes underway in the international financial plumbing than has generally been perceived. Indeed it is arguable that those changes, taken together, amount to a quiet revolution in international financial regulation with, for the first time, the monitoring and compliance muscle of the international financial institutions linked to the standard setting expertise of the regulatory clubs. Much of the framework is now in place; a great deal of work and hard political decisions lies ahead in making it a reality world-wide.

There is no one simple institutional model which can be recommended for universal application. And each country will wish to assess the pros and cons of different structures, in the light of their own financial markets and political structures. The developed countries offer a range of working models from which to choose. What is crucial is to ensure that the regulatory institutions have the independence and authority to take firm, sometimes unpopular decisions in a timely manner. They are there to manage and intermediate risk. They will go up and down, sometimes dramatically.

Conclusion

Irrespective of various challenges, adoption of IFRSs in India has significantly difficult. The contents of corporate financial statements as a result of more refined measurements of performance and state of affairs enhance disclosures leading to greater transparency. With the rapid liberalization process experienced in India over the past decade, there is now a huge presence of multinational enterprises in the country. Furthermore, Indian companies are also investing in foreign markets. This has generated an interest in Indian GAAPs by all concerned. In this context, the role of Indian accounting standards becomes important.

Overall, he concludes, the consequences of adopting a global accounting language should not be considered a done deal yet. "Our findings indicate that the adoption of IFRS has stirred up the process of financial reporting on a worldwide basis," says Hail. "But the lessons and merits of a convergence to global accounting standards and how this affects firms' reporting behaviour on a daily basis are still being debated and will remain a major policy issue for years to come."

REFERENCES

1. International Financial Reporting Standard Setting, http://www.pwc.com/extweb/service.nsf/docid/a01fa5e 222e7060880257126003db26d

2. http://en.wikipedia.org/wiki/International_Financial_Reporting_Standards.

3. Ibid.

4. A Comparison of Generally Accepted Auditing Standards — GAAS and the Generally Accepted Government Auditing Standards — GAGAS (2008) www.academon.com/lib/paper/108032

An assessment of the barriers and challenges to the institution of the International Accounting Standards Board's (IASB) international financial reporting standards (IFRS) (2008) www.academon.com/lib/paper/108033.

5. John Goodwin, Kamran Ahmed Journal (2006), "The Impact of International Financial Reporting Standards: Does Size Matter?" *Managerial Auditing Journal, Volume*: 21, Issue: 5, pp. 460-475.

6. Luzi Hail (2007), Do International Financial Reporting Standards Live Up to Their Promise? November 28, 2007 in Knowledge@Wharton.

7. Luzi Hail and Holger Daske (2007) Mandatory IFRS Reporting Around the World: Early Evidence on the Economic Consequences University of Mannheim, Christian Leuz from the University of Chicago and Rodrigo Verdi MIT.

8. Navin Agrawal (2009), Getting IFRS Right the First Time, Accounting Nuances, Ernst & Young India Pvt. Ltd.

9. International Financial Regulation: The Quiet Revolution, C.D. Deshmukh Memorial Lectures, Reserve Bank of India.

Convergence of Accounting Standard with International Financial Reporting Standards

Jagdish. R. Raiyani

ABSTRACT

The chapter is regarding Convergence of Accounting Standards with International Financial Reporting Standards. It explain the meaning of Accounting Standards and IFRS with it's requirements, benefits and types of challenges faced by the country for converting its Accounting Standards in to IFRS.

Introduction

The Institute of Chartered Accountant of India (ICAI) has decided to converge with IFRSs issued by International Accounting Standards Board from the accounting periods commencing on or after 1st April, 2011. The convergence with IFRS is perceived to be a milestone decision leading to significant benefit to Indian Corporate in terms of easier access to international capital markets, lower cost of capital, improved comparability, elimination of complexities of multiple reporting and many others.

Indian Accounting Standards

In India Accounting Standards (AS) are formulated by Accounting Standard Board (ASB) constituted by the Institute of Chartered Accountants of India (ICAI) in 1977. Indian Accounting Standard may be define as uniform rules for external financial reporting which may be applicable either to all or to a certain class of entity. Till now 32 Accounting Standards has been issued by the ICAI they are as follows:

INDIAN AS NO.	TITLE OF THE INDIAN AS
AS-1	Disclosure of Accounting policies
AS-2	Valuation of Inventories
AS-3	Cash Flow Statement
AS-4	Contingencies and Events Occurring after the Balance sheet date
AS-5	Net profit or loss for the period, prior period items & Changes in Accounting policies.
AS-6	Depreciation Accounting
AS-7	Construction Contracts
AS-8	Accounting for Research & Development
AS-9	Revenue Recognition
AS-10	Accounting for Fixed Assets
AS-11	The Effect of change in Foreign Exchange Rate
AS-12	Accounting for Government Grants
AS-13	Accounting for Investments
AS-14	Accounting for Amalgamations
AS-15	Employee Benefits
AS-16	Borrowing Costs
AS-17	Segment Reporting
AS-18	Related Party Disclosures
AS-19	Leases
AS-20	Earnings per share
AS-21	Consolidated Financial Statements
AS-22	Accounting for Taxes on Income
AS-23	Accounting for Investment in Associates in Consolidated Financial Statements
AS-24	Discontinuing Operations

(Contd...)

AS-25	Interim Financial Reporting
AS-26	Intangible Assets
AS-27	Financial Reporting of Interest in joint venture
AS-28	Impairment of Assets
AS-29	Provisions, Contingent Liabilities and Contingent Assets
AS-30	Financial Instruments Recognition & Measurement
AS-31	Financial Instruments Presentation
AS-32	Financial Instruments Disclosures

International Financial Reporting Standards

International Financial Reporting Standards (IFRS) are principles-based Standards, Interpretations and the Framework[1] adopted by the International Accounting Standards Board (IASB).

Many of the standards forming part of IFRS are known by the older name of International Accounting Standards (IAS). IAS were issued between 1973 and 2001 by the Board of the International Accounting Standards Committee (IASC). On 1 April 2001, the new IASB took over from the IASC the responsibility for setting International Accounting Standards. During its first meeting the new Board adopted existing IAS and SICs. The IASB has continued to develop standards calling the new standards IFRS.

In order to have a standardised procedure and presentation of financial result of different countries, a need arose to have a uniform accounting system, procedure and presentation of accounting results. In order to formulate such an accounting standards, accounting bodies have established a committee called the International Accounting Standard Committee (IASC) in 1973.

From the year 1973 till the year 2001, the IASC laid down various standards known as International Accounting Standards (IAS). However, post 2001 all new standards are called IFRS. Some of the IAS came out as IFRS and rest of IAS still known as IAS. Till date 41 IAS and 8 IFRS are published.

IFRS is adopted by more than 100 countries around the world. Being ICAI of India a member of this body, is going to converge its Indian Accounting Standard into International Financial Reporting Standards.

IFRS has issued following standards:

IFRS-1	First time adoption of IFRSs
IFRS-2	Share based payment
IFRS-3	Business Combinations
IFRS-4	Insurance contracts
IFRS-5	Non-current Assets field for sale & Discontinue operations
IFRS-6	Explorations for and Evaluation of Mineral Assets
IFRS-7	Financial Instrument Disclosure
IFRS-8	Operating segments

Structure of IFRS

IFRS are considered a 'principles based' set of standards in that they establish broad rules as well as dictating specific treatments.

International Financial Reporting Standards comprise:

- International Financial Reporting Standards (IFRS)—standards issued after 2001.
- International Accounting Standards (IAS)—standards issued before 2001.
- Interpretations originated from the International Financial Reporting Interpretations Committee (IFRIC)—issued after 2001.
- Standing Interpretations Committee (SIC)—issued before 2001.
- Framework for the Preparation and Presentation of Financial Statements.

IAS 8 Par. 11

"In making the judgement described in paragraph 10, management shall refer to, and consider the applicability of, the following sources in descending order:

(a) The requirements and guidance in Standards and Interpretations dealing with similar and related issues; and

(b) The definitions, recognition criteria and measurement concepts for assets, liabilities, income and expenses in the Framework."

The Framework for the Preparation and Presentation of Financial Statements states basic principles for IFRS.

The IASB and FASB Frameworks are in the process of being updated and converged. The Joint Conceptual Framework project aims to update and refine the existing concepts to reflect the changes in markets, business practices and the economic environment that have occurred in the two or more decades since the concepts were first developed.

Its overall objective is to create a sound foundation for future accounting standards that are principles-based, internally consistent and internationally converged. Therefore the IASB and the US FASB (the boards) are undertaking the project jointly.

Convergence with IFRS

In simple terms 'Convergence' means to achieve harmony with IFRSs. In precise terms 'Convergence' means to design and maintain national accounting standard in a way that the financial statements prepared in accordance with the national accounting standards draw unreserved statement of compliance with IFRS.

It is not necessary for the economy to adopt IFRS word by word. It is acceptable that if country wants he can add a disclosure according to its requirement or can also remove an optional treatment which will not amount to non-compliance with IFRS.

In pursuance of the statutory mandate provided under the Companies Act, 1956, the Central Government prescribes accounting standards in consultation with the National Advisory Committee on Accounting Standards (NACAS) established under the Companies Act, 1956. NACAS, a body of experts including representatives of various regulatory bodies and Government agencies, has been engaged in the exercise of examining Accounting Standards prepared by ICAI for use by Indian corporate entities, since its constitution in 2001. In this exercise, it has adapted the international norms established by the International Financial Reporting Standards issued by the International Accounting Standards Board.

The Central Government notified 28 Accounting Standards (AS 1 to 7 and AS 9 to 29) in December 2006 in the form of Companies (Accounting Standard) Rules, 2006, after receiving recommendations of NACAS. In notifying the Accounting Standards, the Government has adopted a policy of enabling disclosure of company accounts in a transparent manner at par with widely accepted international practices, through a process of convergence with the International Financial Reporting Standards (IFRS) issued by the International Accounting Standards Board (IASB). In doing so, the requirements of the companies functioning in the country are being kept in view. The initiative for harmonization of the Indian accounting standards with IFRS, taken up by NACAS in 2001 and implemented through notification of accounting standards by the Central Government in 2006, would be continued by the Government with the intention of achieving convergence with IFRS by 2011.

Ministry of Corporate Affairs has also set up a high powered group comprising various stakeholders under the Chairmanship of Shri Anurag Goel, Secretary, to discuss and resolve implementation challenges with regard to convergence of Indian Accounting Standards with International Financial Reporting Standards (IFRS) from the year 2011. The Core Group is supported by two sub-groups. The first sub-group headed by Shri Y.H. Malegam, Chairman, NACAS is to identify changes required in various laws, regulations and accounting standards for convergence with IFRS and to prepare a clear road map for achieving the same. The second sub-group of CFOs under the Chairmanship of Shri Mohandas Pai, Director, Infosys would interact with various stakeholders in order to understand their concerns on the issue of convergence with IFRS, identify problem areas and ascertain the preparedness of the stakeholders for such convergence.

Need for Convergence with IFRS

When all the countries are rushing towards globalisation and liberalisation it is a necessity to have a globally accepted financial reporting system with uniformity, comparability, transparency & adaptability in itself. This will help the user to known only one set of accounting standard to analyse any company in the world.

India has begun its market integration with global financial markets. Companies when crossing National border IFRS make their work easier for capital requirement. Financial statement made under IFRS are accepted by stock exchange all over the world. Hence it facilitates in international business.

Due to Accounting Harmonization the Investors would like to invest directly their capital in efficient companies globally as they properly understand the accounting results of the different companies which lead to more foreign capital flow to the country.

Thus, IFRS, a single set of high quality Accounting Standard removes complexities and confusions of financial statements and also maintain trust of the financial and non-financial users. So due to number of needs convergence with IFRS is required.

The main benefits of IFRS to the adopting countries are as follows:

- It helps the economy to maintain efficient capital market and increase its capital formation.
- Accounting Professionals can provide their service throughout the world.
- IFRS is acceptable by all stock exchange so no multiple reporting.
- It strengthen the confidence of investors so the flow of foreign capital increases.

- It helps the economy to reduce the cost of raising funds.
- It helps in uniformity in reporting to interested groups *i.e* Tax authorities, Researcher etc.

Challenges in Convergence wtih IFRS

Convergence of Accounting Standard into IFRS is not an easy task it has following obstacles on the way of convergence. They are as follows:

- The legal and regulatory requirement of each country is different from each other and Accounting Standard of each country are also different than IFRS. So its a challenging role to change the legal & regulatory requirement according to IFRs;
- Tax law is also different for all the countries;
- Superior complex is also one of the challenge for convergence of Accounting Standards;
- For applicability of IFRS training must be provided to all stake holders, auditors, teachers, students, tax authorities, regulators etc. All the books containing old concepts must be updated accordingly;
- For multinational Companies preparation of financial statements under multiple accounting standards is troublesome and would also cost more;
- There would be practical difficulties for implementing of certain IFRS considering the level of preparedness in the country;
- Companies would have to prepare reconciliation of IFRS Accounts in the first year of its implementation to understand the difference;
- IFRS have conceptual differences with the corresponding Indian Accounting Standard so concept has to be understand properly;
- IFRS have been based on fair value approach which is difficult to be adopted in economic environment of a country like India.

Adoption of IFRS In India

IFRS are used in many parts of the world, including the European Union, Hong Kong, Australia, Malaysia, Pakistan, GCC countries, Russia, South Africa, Singapore and Turkey. As of 27 August 2008, more than 113 countries around the world, including all of Europe, currently require or permit IFRS reporting. Approximately 85 of those countries require IFRS reporting for all domestic, listed companies. In addition, the US is also gearing towards IFRS. The SEC in the US is slowly but progressively shifting from requiring only US GAAP to accepting IFRS and will most likely accept IFRS standards in the long-term.

The Institute of Chartered Accountants of India (ICAI) has announced that IFRS will be mandatory in India for financial statements for the periods beginning on or after 1 April 2011. This will be done by revising existing accounting standards to make them compatible with IFRS. Reserve Bank of India has stated that financial statements of banks need to be IFRS compliant for periods beginning on or after 1 April 2011...

The ICAI has also stated that IFRS will be applied to companies above Rs.1000 crore from April 2011. Phase-wise applicability details for different companies in India:

Phase 1: *Opening Balance Sheet as at 1 April 2011**

i. Companies which are part of NSE Index — Nifty 50

ii. Companies which are part of BSE Sensex — BSE 30

- *a.* Companies whose shares or other securities are listed on a stock exchange outside India
- *b.* Companies, whether listed or not, having net worth of more than INR 1,000 crore

Phase 2: *Opening Balance Sheet as at 1 April 2012**

Companies not covered in phase 1 and having net worth exceeding INR 500 crore

Phase 3: *Opening Balance Sheet as at 1 April 2014**

Listed companies not covered in the earlier phases

* If the financial year of a company commences at a date other than 1 April, then it shall prepare its opening balance sheet at the commencement of immediately following financial year.

On January 22, 2010 the Ministry of Corporate Affairs issued the road map for transition to IFRS. It is clear that India has deferred transition to IFRS by a year. In the first phase, companies included in Nifty 50 or BSE Sensex, and companies whose securities are listed on stock exchanges outside India and all other companies having net worth of Rs 1,000 crore will prepare and present financial statements using Indian Accounting Standards converged with IFRS. According to the press note issued by the government, those companies will convert their first balance sheet as at April 1, 2011, applying accounting standards convergent with IFRS if the accounting year ends on March 31. This implies that the transition date will be April 1, 2011. According to the earlier plan, the transition date was fixed at April 1, 2010.

The press note does not clarify whether the full set of financial statements for the year 2011-12 will be prepared by applying accounting standards convergent with IFRS. The deferment of the transition may make companies happy, but it will undermine India's position. Presumably, lack of preparedness of Indian companies has led to the decision to defer the adoption of IFRS for a year. This is unfortunate that India, which boasts for its IT and accounting skills, could not prepare itself for the transition to IFRS over last four years. But that might be the ground reality. Transition in phases Companies, whether listed or not, having net worth of more than Rs 500 crore will convert their opening balance sheet as at April 1, 2013. Listed companies having net worth of Rs 500 crore or less will convert their opening balance sheet as at April 1, 2014. Unlisted companies having net worth of Rs 500 crore or less will continue to apply existing accounting standards, which might be modified from time to time. Transition to IFRS in phases is a smart move. The transition cost for smaller companies will be much lower because large companies will bear the initial cost of learning and smaller companies will not be required to reinvent the wheel. However, this will happen only if a significant number of large companies engage Indian accounting firms to provide them support in their transition to IFRS. If, most large companies, which will comply with Indian accounting standards convergent with IFRS in the first phase, choose one of the international firms, Indian accounting firms and smaller companies will not benefit from the learning in the first phase of the transition to IFRS. It is likely that international firms will protect their learning to retain their competitive advantage. Therefore, it is for the benefit of the country that each company makes judicious choice of the accounting firm as its partner without limiting its choice to international accounting firms. Public sector companies should take the lead and the Institute of Chartered Accountants of India (ICAI) should develop a clear strategy to diffuse the learning.

Size of Companies: The government has decided to measure the size of companies in terms of net worth. This is not the ideal unit to measure the size of a company. Net worth in the balance sheet is determined by accounting principles and methods. Therefore, it does not include the value of intangible assets. Moreover, as most assets and liabilities are measured at historical cost, the net worth does not reflect the current value of those assets and liabilities. Market capitalisation is a better measure of the size of a company. But it is difficult to estimate market capitalisation or fundamental value of unlisted companies. This might be the reason that the government has decided to use 'net worth' to measure size of companies. Some companies, which are large in terms of fundamental value or which intend to attract foreign capital, might prefer to use Indian accounting standards convergent with IFRS earlier than required under the road map presented by the government. The government should provide that choice. The government will come up with a separate road map for banking and insurance companies by February 28, 2010. Let us hope that transition in case of those companies will not be deferred further.

Conclusion

In this chapter an attempt has been made to explain meaning, need and challenges of convergence of Accounting Standard with IFRS. For the convergence of Accounting Standard with IFRS people is required to change their mindset and accept the change as early as possible to have better growth of economy. It should be made mandatory by law for every country to implement IFRS as fast as possible. Irrespective of various challenges adoption of IFRS in India is significant for more refined measurement of performance and state of affairs.

REFERENCES

1. Lantto, Anna-Maija and Sahlström, Petri (2009), Impact of International Financial Reporting Standard Adoption on Key Financial Ratios, *Accounting and Finance*, 49, 341-361.
2. Armstrong, Chris S., Barth, Mary E., Jagolinzer, Alan D. and Riedl, Edward J. (2009), Market Reaction to the Adoption of IFRS in Europe, *Accounting Review Forthcoming.*
3. Ball, Ray (2005), International Financial Reporting Standards (IFRS): Pros and Cons for Investors, *Accounting and Business Research, Forthcoming.*
4. Daske, Holger, Hail, Luzi, Leuz, Christian and Verdi, Rodrigo S. (2008), Mandatory IFRS Reporting Around the World: Early Evidence on the Economic Consequences. ECGI — *Finance Working Paper No. 198/2008; Chicago GSB Research Paper No. 12.*
5. De Jong, Abe, Rosellón Cifuentes, Miguel Angel and Verwijmeren, Patrick (2006), The Economic Consequences of IFRS: The Impact of IAS 32 on Preference Shares in the Netherlands, *ERIM Report Series* Reference No. ERS-2006-021-F&A.
6. Hboxma (2008), Economics and IFRS, Retrieved on October 14, 2009 from http://www.oppapers.com/essays/Economics-Ifrs/177415.
7. Callao, Susana, Ferrer, Cristina, Jarne, Jose I. and Lainez, Jose A. (2009), The Impact of IFRS on the European Union: Is It Related to the Accounting Tradition of the Countries?, *Journal of Applied Accounting Research,* 10(1), 33-55.
8. Carmona, Salvador and Trombetta, Marco (2008), On the Global Acceptance of IAS/IFRS Accounting Standards: The Logic and Implications of the Principles-based System, *Journal of Accounting and Public Policy,* 27(6).

9. "Concept paper on Convergence with IFRSs in India" (2007) The Institute of Chartered Accountant of India.
10. Shri Asish. K. Bhattacharya "*Indian Accounting Standards*".
11. "*International Financial Reporting Standards*" Taxmann India Publications Pvt. Ltd.
12. www.icai.org
13. www.iasplus.com
14. www.iasb.org

Corporate Disclosure
Need for Transparency

Mr. Suresh Sahoo,
Dr. S.K. Chaudhury

"Between my past, the present and future, there is one factor — relationship and trust. This is the foundation of our growth"

— **Dhirubhai Mantra**

ABSTRACT

Corporate governance is all about ethical conduct in business. Ethics is concerned with the code of values and principles that enables a person to choose between right and wrong, and therefore, select from alternative courses of action. Further, ethical dilemmas arise from conflicting interests of the parties involved. In this regard, managers make decisions based on a set of principles influenced by the values, context and culture of the organization. Ethical leadership is good for business as the organization is seen to conduct its business in line with the expectations of all stakeholders. What constitutes good Corporate Governance will evolve with the changing circumstances of a company and must be tailored to meet these circumstances. There is therefore no one single model of Corporate Governance.

Introduction

The ongoing wave of liberalization and globalization sweeping across the world has opened many domestic markets for international business. The forces of liberalization and globalization have led to a surge in the business volume in the last couple of decades, highlighting the need for greater awareness and vigilance, scrutiny and transparency in the corporate world. These forces have also led to unprecedented changes in the corporate domain and have been instrumental in creating innovative means for communicating financial information to the market place. The field of services sector has witnessed remarkable advance resulting in dramatic changes in the way business is being transacted all over the world. The expansion of global markets has also influenced the movement of funds across countries. Innovative financial instruments have been evolved to deal with new global economic realities and a more complex business environment. When the international business environment is undergoing rapid transformation and new linkages are sought to be enforced through multilateral trade negotiations, there is a need for restructuring the industry, agriculture and other sectors of economy to meet new challenges in the changing global business scenario. As a result, corporate reporting has also undergone a sea change, presenting newer challenges and further opportunities.

Corporate disclosure is of great significance in the accomplishment of financial accounting objectives and in contributing to the efficient allocation of resources through sound economic decisions. The quality of corporate disclosure influences to a great extent the quality of investment decisions made by the investors.

Globalisation is a continuous process; at the most basic level, a purely domestic company's ability to compete is influenced by changes in foreign exchange rates, technological advances, cultural diversity, and international political and economic issues. An example of a high level globalisation is a multinational enterprise whose production and sales locations span multiple foreign locations from raw materials extraction to final product assembly and sales (Ex. Iron ore of Orissa origin being taking shape of automobiles with assembly line at Japan/Korea).

In the regime of globalized business, every corporate management releases its story into different media. Contextually every manager should be careful to make its story strictly non-fiction keeping the goal not is to put investors to a slumber, but rather to make the information it is conveying to investors compelling and understandable. Recent high profile corporate failures have yet again focussed world-wide attention on the importance of disclosure and corporate accountability. These failures have emphasized that disclosure of information must not only be timely but complete, clear and accurate.

Prima-facie three broad sector of reporting can ignite interest of stakeholders into corporate happenings so as to extend proactive suggestions, most important stakeholder being the auditors:

- *Investor Centric Reporting:* The traditional performance reporting formats are biased towards historic information and is short term oriented. It needs to realign for explaining long term value potential of the business;
- Inclusion of contextual and non-financial information on the business.
- *Internal Control over Financial Reporting Having Effective Deterrents against Frauds*: prevention of financial misstatements with the Board/CEO/CFO of the enterprise taking ownership over preparation of the financial statements and its presentation.

The above three being broad pre-requisites, the management can most effectively tell its story through the Management Discussion and Analysis, the MD&A and at the same time making the financials more understandable and compelling by putting focus on accounting for the substance of transactions.

While the system of financial reporting is a function of the economic, legal and political institutions in a country, the changes taking place in the commercial world due to globalisation have resulted in accountancy profession critically reviewing its role and relevance of its curriculum.

In early times accounting was merely concerned with ascertainment of results of business enterprises. But, financial reporting has a new orientation these days owing to the increased needs of users accounting information.

The Indian Scenario

The global trend is to move towards uniform accounting principles in view of opening up of the world trade. The set of accounting principles and standards not only guides appropriate accounting treatment of complex business transactions but also provide, new concepts, which may be applied to different business situations. The global standardization of accounting issues is of vital importance in this era of cross-border movement of capital. The process of globalisation, issue of corporate reporting, deregulations and the consequential accounting standards changes have impacted Indian scenario as well. In the light of corporate failures, financial irregularities and lack of adequate management accountability, it is looked upon as a distinctive brand and benchmark in the profile of corporate excellence.

There have been major changes in financial reporting in India since the economic reforms and globalisation began in the early 1990s. The two major driving force behind these changes are:

Pressure of Capital, Product and Labour Market

Pressure of capital market became evident as Indian Companies depended to a greater extent on the capital market for raising resources since the year 1991. Further, financial reporting has been influenced by FI investment, FDI, disinvestments and privatisation, and listing in overseas stock exchanges. A product market pressure arises from the greater interactions of Indian firms with overseas market in the form of exports and imports of goods and services since the commencement of economic reforms. The overseas customers, dealing with Indian firms, are concerned with the firm's financial performance, and they demand superior quality financial reports to monitor the firm's performance. Pressure from labour market is another important factor for compelling the recent changes. Indian firms need talent to stay ahead of the competition in their product and capital markets. Superior financial reporting could be useful in convincing a firm's present and potential employees of its financial soundness, so that the key users of a firm's accounting information they can trust the firm as a dependable employer offering good long-term prospects of growth.

1. Company law and securities law amendments
2. International accounting and securities regulations

Company Law and Securities Law Amendments

In the last decade, there has been a significant change in Indian Laws and regulatory requirements relating to accounting and governance. In 1999, the Companies Act 1956 was amended to provide for setting up of NACAS (National Advisory Committee on Accounting Standards) to advise government on formulation of accounting standards. Also SEBI has, over the years played an active role in requiring compliance with accounting standards, made cash flow reporting mandatory through listing agreement, further required segment reporting in listed companies' quarterly results. Another significant reform has been in the area of corporate governance. The recommendations of various committees on corporate governance like the Narayana Murthy Committee, Naresh Chandra Committee, the Kumar Mangalam Birla Committee etc. contributed substantially to the monitoring of quality of financial statements.

The impact of globalisation of the Indian Economy on reporting practices is already becoming visible. The Indian Scenario in the matter of evolution and adoption of accounting standards, of late, is rapid. The important developments in Indian financial reporting to cope with the globalisation is: *(i)* Introduction of new Indian Accounting Standards such as Segment reporting, Related party disclosure, lease accounting, interim finance accounting, reporting on intangible assets and host of other issues.

The Companies Act 1956, has been amended extensively through the Companies (Amendment) Act, 2000. As far as new listing agreements are concerned, SEBI has made it mandatory for appending of cash flow statements.

Some new dimensions of financial reporting include : value added statement, HRA, social reporting, and certain emerging areas like value reporting, corporate sustainability reporting, governance reporting etc.

Role of SEBI in Corporate Disclosure in—Case of Right Issues

SEBI's recent board meeting has resulted in certain significant decisions impacting capital markets activity in India as well as SEBI's own decision-making process.

1. *SEBI to Extend Validity of the Observation Letter*

   SEBI Board has approved extension of validity of observation letter issued for public/rights issue from present three months to one year, subject to filing of updated document with SEBI where there are material changes.

2. *SEBI to Introduce Electronic rights Entitlements and ASBA in the Rights Issue Process*

   SEBI Board has approved certain policy measures pertaining to rights issue process, which inter-alia include enabling electronic rights entitlement, which can be traded electronically in Stock Exchanges, introducing alternate mode for making applications in rights issue viz Applications Supported by Blocked Amount (ASBA) mode and mandating that the issuer can get access to rights issue proceeds only after the allotment is finalized.

Currently a shareholder intending to renounce his/her Rights entitlements fills up part B of the rights issue application form. The renouncee can trade this form or apply in the Rights Issue by filling up Part C of the form. Renunciation forms are traded in physical segment in Bombay Stock Exchange. The right entitlement will now be made available in demat form for all shareholders holding the underlying shares in demat form.

The policy measures approved by the Board in this meeting, along with measures undertaken in the recent past for reduction in time lines, are expected to streamline the rights issue process and make it more efficient.

3. It was decided that no early exit will be allowed in any scheme of Mutual Fund in the nature of a close ended scheme. The schemes which have been approved earlier but not yet launched will also have to be amended accordingly. It will

be obligatory for the Asset Management Company to list the close ended schemes. The Board also decided that for such close ended schemes the underlying assets will not have a maturity beyond the date on which the scheme expires.

4. The Board decided to adopt a code to avoid conflict of interest for the members of the Board. It was further decided that this code will be put up in the public domain by publishing it on the SEBI website before December 12, 2008.

SEBI has, over the years, been introducing transparency in its regulatory process. For instance, it has been following the practice of issuing policy papers on key changes to regulations and seeking comments before the actual regulations are enacted. This current measure is a further step in that direction, and has received a favourable response generally. Perhaps this may also provide a suitable model for other Indian regulators to emulate.

Another related decision (on stock exchanges and the use of RTI to seek information) bolsters the element of transparency. The Economic Times reports:

Gaining access to information relating to the securities market will now be easier, with the Securities and Exchange Board of India (SEBI) taking the view that it has the authority to seek information from stock exchanges for providing it to the public under the Right to Information Act (RTI).

India's main stock exchanges such as the Bombay Stock Exchange (BSE) and the National Stock Exchange (NSE) were reluctant to provide information saying they are not a public authority under RTI. A recent ruling by the appellate authority of the market regulator has stated that stock exchanges are bound to furnish information sought by the regulator even if it is for the RTI purpose.

With companies preferring other modes of raising capital post IPO, the market regulator SEBI today proposed relaxing the disclosure norms for rights issues to help shareholders retain their stake and reduce overall cost of issuance.

"Rights issues are further issuance of capital made by listed entities to its existing shareholders. Certain information about the entities that are listed and traded on the exchanges is available in the public domain," SEBI said in a discussion paper while making a case for less disclosures for rights issues.

SEBI said it may not be necessary to mandate exhaustive disclosure requirements.

"In such cases it may suffice to have a more restricted set of disclosures about the issue and the entity," SEBI said while inviting comments from the public by March 28.

The market regulator pointed out that quite often issuers choose preferential offers or qualified institutional placements or even ADR and GDR issuances over rights issues as these modes require less time, cost and efforts.

These alternate modes other than rights issues while helping the entities to achieve the capital raising needs, dilutes the existing shareholders stake in the entity.

The market regulator added that rationalisation of disclosure norms for rights issues would not only make the issuance process faster but also contribute to savings in paper, printing and distribution costs, reducing overall cost of issuance.

The SEBI Committee on Disclosures and Accounting Standards (SCODA) has recommended seperate set of disclosures for rights issues provided the listed company has been filing periodical statements for the last three years and has investor grievance handling mechanism with regard to share transfer.

SEBI recently ammended guidelines relating to time lines for rights issues resulting in reduction of more than two months in the process of coming out with such offers.

The market regulator, Securities and Exchange Board of India (SEBI), in an effort to enhance the efficiency of primary markets, has reduced the time frame for completion of rights issues. In order to achieve the same, it has decided to amend the SEBI disclosure and Investment protection (DIP) guidelines and the Listing Agreement. However, contrary to expectation, no decision on restrictions on issue of Participatory Notes by FIIs was taken by the market regulator today.

Reduction in timeline approved include: the number of days for the notice period for a board meeting to be reduced from 7 days to 2 working days; the notice period for record date to be reduced from 15/21/30 days to 7 working days for all scrips; issue period will be reduced from minimum 30 days to minimum 15 days with a maximum of 30 days and the time period for completion of post issue activity will be reduced from 42 days to 15 days.

These changes in timeline would enable a right issue to be completed within about 43 days as against about 109 days currently available for a rights issue.

The reduction in time lines would reduce the market risk faced by investors and issuers and would ensure faster turnaround of money for investors.

SEBI has also revised the pricing norms for qualified institutional placement (QIP) and preferential allotment. According to the revision, floor price may be based on the two weeks average for making a QIP or for making preferential allotment to qualified institutional buyers (QIBs). Currently QIP and preferential allotment require that the floor price for issue of securities shall be higher of the average of the weekly high and low of the closing prices of the shares during the two weeks or six months preceding the relevant date.

Further, SEBI board approved the modification to Clause 41 of the listing agreement, under which the time limit for submission of financial results to stock exchanges has been revised. As per the revision, a listed entity in addition to submitting quarterly and year to date standalone financial results within one month of end of the quarter may also submit consolidated financial results to the stock exchange within two months from the end of the quarter.

Additionally, the board approved the reduction in time period for dispatch of Annual Report to the mutual fund unit holders. The mutual funds would now be required to disclose their results within four months of the end of the fiscal instead of six months currently. The new norm will come into effect from 2008-09.

SEBI Eases Disclosure Norms for Debt Issues

In a move that will streamline the process of corporate bond issues, the Securities and Exchange Board of India (SEBI) has put out a draft listing agreement for the issuance of debt securities, prepared in consultation with the Bombay Stock Exchange (BSE) and National Stock Exchange (NSE).

The disclosures in the draft listing agreement are based on the principle that if an issuer's equity is already listed, such an issuer only makes minimal incremental disclosures specific to the debt issuance.

In cases where only the debt securities are listed, reasonably elaborate disclosures, albeit lesser than equity, are prescribed. The draft will be available on the SEBI website till August 25 for public comments.

The listing agreement has two parts — Part A has 8 clauses and is applicable to issuers whose equity shares are already listed on the exchanges. Part B, having 19 clauses, is applicable to issuers whose equity shares are not listed on the exchange.

An issuer complying with Part B would move to Part A compliance whenever the equity shares get listed. Similarly, an issuer delisting equity would need to comply with Part B.

Further, the Corporate Bonds and Securitisation Advisory Committee (CoBoSAC) under the chairmanship of Dr RH Patil, has recommended the mandatory DvP-111 clearing and settlement on exchanges with Real Time Gross Settlement (RTGS).

The committee has suggested a sub-group to look into issues pertaining to trade reporting.. SEBI had first proposed draft regulations for simplifying the corporate bond issuances in January this year.

Conclusion

In the present era of globalisation, the basic contours of reporting business performance have been changing at a fast pace. The dramatic changes in the Indian economy have been influencing the different aspects of the corporate sector. True success of a business entity is in the truthful expression of the performance when it is measured. A general perception is that financial reporting practices have improved over the past 5 years; however, significantly strengthened enforcement mechanisms are needed to further improve the quality of corporate financial reporting. The fast pace of globalisation resulted in Indian accounting standards and corporate governance requirements are in line with international practices. But India is still in the early stages of its involvement in the globalisation of accounting standards. With the global economy changing rapidly, more and more Indian companies need to march towards attaining global standards.

REFERENCES

1. http://www.blonnet.com/2009/03/13/stories/2009031351561000.htm
2. www.sebi.gov.in/circulars/2008
3. www.scribd.com/doc/190274/-INDIAS-SEBI-STRIKING-THE-HAMMER
4. www.business-standard.com/india/news/sebi-eases-disclosure-norms-for-debt-issues/331800/
5. indiacorplaw.blogspot.com/2008/12/self-regulation-for-directors-on-sebis.html
6. www.domain-b.com/investments/markets/sebi/index.html
7. www.palgrave-journals.com/jdg/journal/v5/n3/full/jdg20089a.html

Challenges of International Financial Reporting Standards and Its Applicability in India

Prof. Trilok Nath Shukla,
Miss. Archita De

ABSTRACT

In line with the global trend, the Institute of Chartered Accountants of India (ICAI) proposed a plan for convergence with International Financial Reporting Standards (IFRS) for certain defined entities — including banks — with effect from April 1, 2011. Convergence to IFRS would mean India would join a league of more than 100 countries, which have converged with IFRS. This process is likely to entail several changes to financial reporting which would need to be planned, managed, tested and executed in advance of the implementation date. The Indian GAAP has conceptual differences with IFRS and our legal and regulatory frameworks need to be amended for us to adopt IFRS as written by the International Accounting Standards Board, the standard setting body of IFRS. Indian corporates are likely to reap significant benefits from adopting IFRS. The European Union's experience highlights many perceived benefits as a result of adopting IFRS. In this chapter we have tried to cover all the aspects of IFRS and also the challenges which we will face in implementing this system in India.

Keywords: IFRS, International Accounting Standards Board, GAAP, Accounting Standards, Investments.

Introduction

The growing acceptance of International Financial Reporting Standards (IFRS) as a basis for U.S. financial reporting represents a fundamental change for the U.S. accounting profession. Today nearly 100 countries require or allow the use of IFRS for the preparation of financial statements by publicly held companies. In the United States, the Securities and Exchange Commission (SEC) is considering taking steps to set a date to allow U.S. public companies to use IFRS, and perhaps make its adoption mandatory.

The international standard-setting process began several decades ago as an effort by industrialized nations to create standards that could be used by developing and smaller nations unable to establish their own accounting standards. But as the business world became more global, regulators, investors, large companies and auditing firms began to realize the importance of having common standards in all areas of the financial reporting chain.

World-wide Momentum

The globalization of business and finance has led more than 12,000 companies in almost a hundred countries to adopt IFRS. In 2005, the European Union (EU) began requiring companies incorporated in its member states whose securities are listed on an EU-regulated stock exchange to prepare their consolidated financial statements in accordance with IFRS1. Australia, New Zealand and Israel have essentially adopted IFRS as their national standards. Canada, which previously planned convergence with U.S. Generally Accepted Accounting Principles (GAAP) now plans to require IFRS for publicly accountable entities in 2011. The Accounting Standards Board of Japan (ASBJ) and the International Accounting Standards Board (IASB) plan convergence by 2011.

What is International Financial and Reporting Standards (IFRS)?

IFRS is an accounting framework that establishes recognition, measurement, presentation and disclosure requirements relating to transactions and events that are reflected in the financial statements. IFRS was developed in the year 2001 by the International Accounting Standards Board (IASB) in the public interest to provide a single set of high quality, understandable and uniform accounting standards.

Need for IFRS

- To make a common platform for better understanding of accounting, internationally.
- Synchronization of accounting standards across the globe.
- To create comparable, reliable, and transparent financial statements.
- To facilitate greater cross-border capital raising and trade.
- To having company-wide one accounting language which have subsidiaries in different countries.

Objectives of IFRS

- To develop a single set of accounting standards.

  (High quality, understandable, global and enforceable).
- To promote their use and rigorous application.
- To work actively with national standard setters (To bring about convergence of national accounting standards and IFRSs).

However in a survey conducted recently by the International Federation of Accountants (IFAC), a large majority of accounting leaders from around the world agreed that a single set of international standards is important for economic growth. Of the 143 leaders from 91 countries who responded, 90 per cent reported that a single set of international financial reporting standards was 'very important' or 'important' for economic growth in their countries. This is shown in Graph No.6.1. (*see on next page*)

The U.S. Securities and Exchange Commission has for many years been a strong leader in international efforts to develop a core set of accounting standards that could serve as a framework for financial reporting in cross-border offerings. It has repeatedly

With respect of the importance of convergence to International Financial Reporting Standards for economic growth in their counties:

- 55 per cent of respondents said IFRS adoption was 'very important' to economic growth

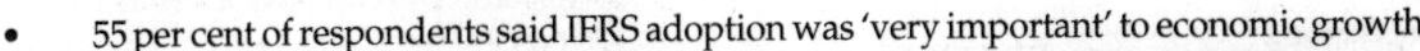

- 35 per cent said 'important'
- 9 per cent 'some what important'
- 1 per cent 'not important'

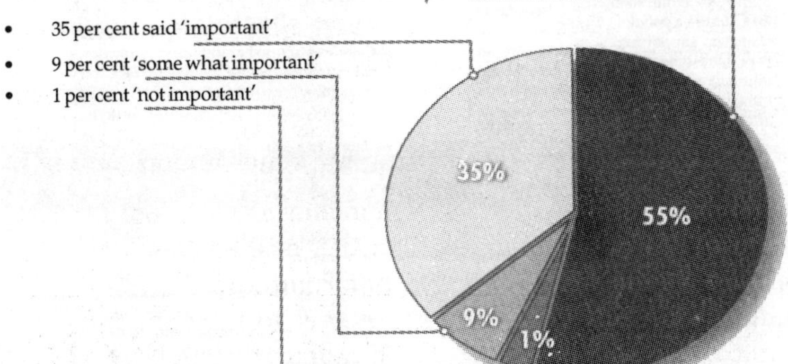

Graph No. 6.1

Source: www.ifrs.com/updates/aicpa/Backgrounder_pdf.html

made the case that issuers wishing to raise capital in more than one country are faced with the increased compliance costs and inefficiencies of preparing multiple sets of financial statements to comply with different jurisdictional accounting requirements. In 2000, the International Organization of Securities Commissions (IOSCO), in which the SEC plays a leading role, recommended that its members allow multinational issuers to use 30 'core' standards issued by the IASB's predecessor body in cross-border offerings and listings. The developments are shown by following graph no. 6.2. (*see on next page*)

Growing interest in the global acceptance of a single set of robust accounting standards comes from all participants in the capital markets. Many multinational companies and national regulators and users support it because they believe that the use of common standards in the preparation of public company financial statements will make it easier to compare the financial results of reporting entities from different countries. They believe it will help investors understand opportunities better. Large public companies with subsidiaries in multiple jurisdictions would be able to use one accounting language company-wide and present their financial statements in the same language as their competitors.

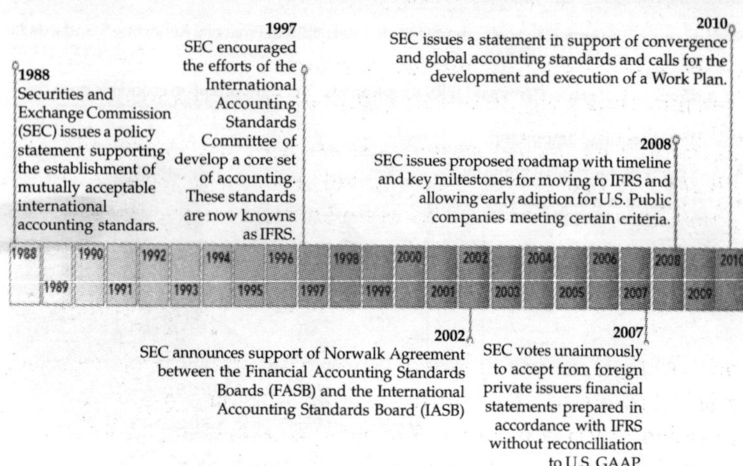

Graph No. 6.2

Source: www.ifrs.com/updates/aicpa/Backgrounder_pdf.html

Another benefit some believe is that in a truly global economy, financial professionals including CPAs will be more mobile, and companies will more easily be able to respond to the human capital needs of their subsidiaries around the world.

Nevertheless, many people also believe that U.S. GAAP is the gold standard, and something will be lost with full acceptance of IFRS. What's more, it is unlikely that all U.S. issuers will voluntarily elect to use IFRS.

Another concern is that world-wide, many countries that claim to be converging to international Standards may never get to 100 per cent compliance. Most reserve the right to carve out electively or modify standards they do not consider in their national interest, an action that could lead to incomparability—the very issue that IFRS seek to address.

Background

2001: The International Accounting Standards Board (IASB) is established as the successor organization to the International Accounting Standards Committee (IASC), formed in 1973. 2002: The IASB and the Financial Accounting Standards Board (FASB) issue the Norwalk Agreement, acknowledging their joint commitment to developing high quality, compatible accounting standards that could be used for both domestic and cross-border financial reporting. Also, the European Union (EU) announces that its member states will require IFRS in the preparation of consolidated financial statements of listed companies beginning in 2005.

2005

The chief accountant of the Securities and Exchange Commission (SEC) releases a roadmap allowing IFRS filings without GAAP reconciliation for foreign firms by 2009.

2006

The IASB and the FASB agree to work on a number of major projects.

2007

The SEC announces that it will accept from foreign filers in the U.S. financial statements prepared in accordance with IFRS, as issued by the IASB, without reconciliation to U.S. GAAP. Also, the SEC issues a Concept Release asking if U.S. public companies should be given an option to follow IFRS instead of U.S. GAAP.

2008

The SEC is expected to vote on a proposal creating a timeline for moving U.S. public companies to IFRS. The AICPA's governing Council considers amending rules 202 and 203 of the Code of Professional Conduct to recognize the IASB as an international accounting standard setter, thereby giving U.S. private companies and not-for-profit organizations a choice to follow IFRS. Also, the FASB and the IASB update the Norwalk Agreement with the goal of accelerating convergence.

2009

The IASB will end its moratorium, set in 2005, on the required application of new accounting standards and major amendments to existing standards. The board had frozen its rules while more countries adopted IFRS.

2011

Canadian and Indian companies are slated to begin using the global standards, and Japan is slated to have eliminated all major differences between Japanese GAAP and IFRS. In the United States, questions concerning IFRS are expected to be included in the Uniform CPA Exam.

2013

The earliest year projected by accounting firms for mandating that large U.S. public companies convert their financials to IFRS. Year that the updated Norwalk Agreement expects all major capital markets to operate from one set of accounting standards capital markets to operate from one set of accounting standards.

A compact picture of it is shown in Graph No. 6.3 below:

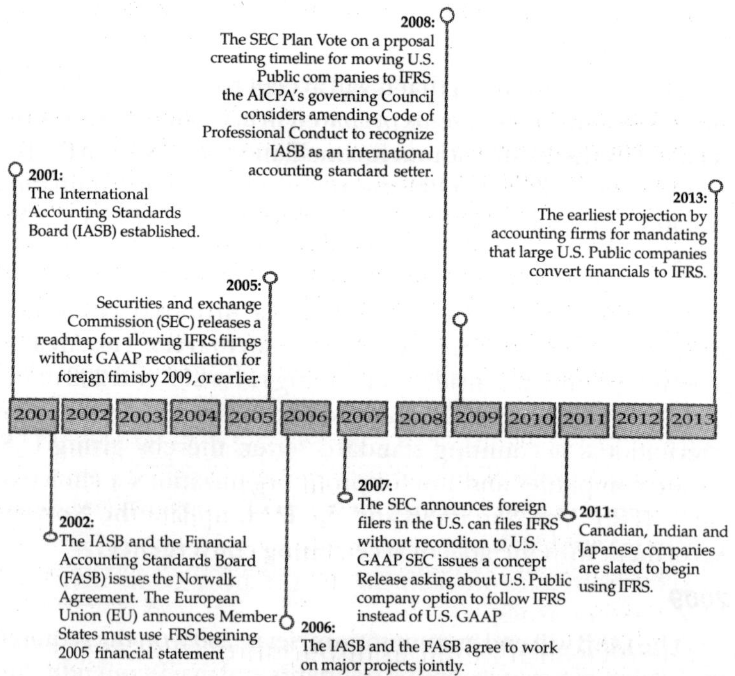

Graph No. 6.3

Source: www.ifrs.com/updates/aicpa/Backgrounder_pdf.html

Setting Accounting Standards in India A Historical Perspective

India's accounting profession was among the earliest to develop after the introduction of the Indian Companies Act in the mid -1800, giving the accounting profession its start . Indian accounting and auditing standards are developed on the basis of international standards; and the country has many accountants and auditors who are highly skilled and capable of providing international-standard services.

GAAP is the abbreviation of Generally Accepted Accounting Principle. AAP are the common set of accounting principles, standars and procedures that companies use to compile their financial statements. In India, GAAP standards are set by the Institute of Chartered Accountants (ICAI) in 1982. ICAI continually updates GAAP as new accounting issues and concerns arise. GAAP are imposed on companies so that investors have a minimum level of consistency in the financial statements they use when analyzing companies for investment purposes. GAAP cover such things as revenue recognition, balance sheet item classification and outstanding share measurements. Since GAAP is only a set of guidelines, it cannot guarantee financial statements are not fraudulent. So, even when a company uses GAAP, we still need to scrutinize its financial statements.

While formulating accounting standards in India, the ASB considers International Financial Reporting Standards (IFRS) and tries to integrate them, to the extent possible, in the light of the laws, customs, practices and business environment prevailing in India. ICAI interacts with the IASB at various levels, namely:

- Sending comments on the various draft IFRSs issued by IASB;
- Active participation in the meetings of the global standard-setters with IASB;
- Active participation in the meeting of the regional standard-setters with IASB;
- Contribution in the discussions on various ongoing projects of the IASB, *e.g.* IASB management commentary project;
- ICAI is approaching IASB to take up projects to be carried on by India, *e.g.* IFRS for regulated enterprises.

IFRS and Indian Corporates

- The use of international financial reporting standards (IFRS) as a universal financial reporting language is gaining momentum across the globe.
- The Institute of Chartered Accountants of India (ICAI) has recently released a concept paper on Convergence with IFRS in India, detailing the strategy for adoption of IFRS in India with effect from April 1, 2011. This has been strengthened by a recent announcement from the Ministry of Corporate Affairs (MCA) confirming the agenda for convergence with IFRS in India by 2011.
- Adopting IFRS by Indian corporate is going to be very challenging but at the same time could also be rewarding. Indian corporate is likely to reap significant benefits from adopting IFRS.

Benefits of IFRS on Indian Corporates

- Improvement in comparability of financial information and financial performance with global peers and industry standards.
- Adoption of IFRS is expected to result in better quality of financial reporting due to consistent application of accounting principles and improvement in reliability of financial statements.
- Better access to and reduction in the cost of capital raised from global capital market since IFRS are now accepted as a financial reporting framework for companies seeking to raise funds from most capital markets across the globe.

Guidelines

- Understanding and analyzing the impact of IFRS on financial performance.
- Obtaining the new data required and adapting systems to provide it.
- Finding the resources and expertise needed to make the changes.

- Meeting employee training and knowledge sharing needs.
- Aligning systems for reporting for statutory, regulatory and internal purposes.
- Gaining shareholder and analyst understanding of the impact of changing to IFRS.

Regulatory Framework

(A) Legal Recognition of Accounting Standards issued by ICAI under the Companies Act(1956)

The Companies Act (1956) requires the preparation, presentation, publication, and disclosure of financial statements, as well as an audit of all companies by a member-in-practice certified by the Institute of Chartered Accountants of India (ICAI). Under the Act, the Central Government has the power, by notification in the Official Gazette, to constitute the National Advisory Committee on Accounting Standards (NACAS), to advise the Central Government on the formulation and laying down of accounting standards for adoption by companies or class of companies. For this purpose, the act requires that NACAS has to consider accounting standards issued by the ICAI when recommending accounting standards to the government. NACAS also specifically considers the deviations- and reasons, if any- from the corresponding IAS/IFRS while reviewing ICAI accounting standards. In case the NACAS is not satisfied about any deviation, it requests ICAI to amend the standard to comply with IFRS. ICAI generally deviates from the corresponding IAS/IFRS because of the following factors:

- Legal and regulatory environment prevailing in the country;
- Alternatives permitted in IFRS would lead to incomparable financial information;
- Economic environment within the country;
- Level of preparedness of industry.

NACAS has recommended that all 29 accounting standards issued by ICAI, with the exception of AS 8, Accounting for Research and Development , which has already been withdrawn pursuant to AS 26, Intangible Assets, Becoming mandatory, to the government, for notification under the Companies Act (1956). These include the revised AS 15, Employee Benefits, recently issued by ICAI in line with IAS 19, Employee Benefits. These are expected to be notified by the Government shortly. Until then, the companies act (1956) specifically provides that ICAI accounting standards need to be adhered to by companies.

(B) Legal Recognition of Accounting Standards by Other Regulators

i. Reserve Bank of India

The Reserve Bank of India (RBI) was established to regulate the issue of bank notes and keeping reserves to secure monetary stability in India, as well as to generally operate the currency and credit system of the country to its advantage.

ii. Securities and Exchange Board of India

Listed companies in India are required to comply with the requirements prescribed by the SEBI in its Act of 1992 and the Securities Contract (Regulation) Act of 1956, which provides for the regulation of securities transaction,. To protect investor interest, SEBI has issued a listing agreement which specifies disclosures applicable to listed companies in addition to other applicable auditing and accounting requirements. In particular, it requires compliance with the accounting standards issued by ICAI.

iii. The Insurance Regulatory and Development Authority (IRDA)

This Authority has been constituted to regulate, promote and ensure orderly growth of the insurance business and reinsurance business. Insurance companies and their auditors are required to comply with the requirements of the IRDA regulations of 2002 titled "Preparations of Financial Statements and Auditor's Report of the Insurance Companies", in preparing and presenting their financial statements and the format and content of the audit report. IRDA regulations require compliance with the accounting standards issued by ICAI.

iv. The Institute of Chartered Accountants of India as a Regulator

The ICAI requires its members to ensure compliance with all the accounting standards it issues while discharging their attest functional and the members are also required to follow a detailed Code of Ethics, as prescribed under the Chartered Accountants Act, (1949). The ICAI council is also entrusted with the disciplinary powers that are exercised through its Disciplinary Committee. Recently, extensive changes have been made in the act though The Chartered Accountants (Amendment) Act, 2006, which has made the disciplinary mechanism of the ICAI more stringent. The ICAI has also constituted the financial reporting review board (FRRB) which reviews general purpose financial statements of certain selected enterprises with a view to check compliance, inter alia, with the accounting standards.

Differences between IFRS and Indian GAAP

(a) Conceptual Accounting Framework

Historical Cost

IFRS

Historical cost, but intangible assets, property plant and equipment (PPE) and investment property may be revalued. Derivatives, biological assets and most securities must be revalued.

Indian GAAP

Historical cost, but fixed assets, other than intangibles, may be revalue.

First-time Adoption of Accounting Frameworks

IFRS

Full retrospective application of all IFRS's effective at the reporting date for an entity's first IFRS financial statements, with some optional exemptions and limited mandatory exceptions.

Indian GAAP

The accounting standard on Disclosure of Accounting Policies addresses the issue of adoption of accounting policies. Also, particular standards specify the transitional treatment upon the first-time application of those standards.

Contents of Financial Statements

IFRS

Two years' balance sheets, income statements, cash-flow statements, changes in equity, accounting policies and notes.

Indian GAAP

Two years' balance sheets, profit and loss accounts, accounting policies and notes. Listed entities are required to give their consolidated financial statements and the related notes along with the standalone financial statements. (Financial Statements should also include cash flow statements in certain cases.

IFRS

Does not prescribe a particular format; an entity uses a liquidity presentation of assets and liabilities, instead of a current/non-current presentation, only when a liquidity presentation provides more relevant and reliable information. Certain items must be presented on the face of the balance sheet.

Indian GAAP

The Indian Companies Act and other industry-specific laws like banking, insurance, etc. specify respective formats.

Income Statements

IFRS

Does not prescribe a particular format. However, expenditure must be presented in one of two formats (function or nature). Certain items must be presented on the face of the income statement.

Indian GAAP

The Indian Companies Act does not prescribe a particular format. The Company law and accounting standards however, prescribes certain disclosure norms for income and expenditures. For certain industries, industry specific laws specify formats.

Reporting Currency

IFRS

Requires the measurement of profit using the functional currency. Entities may, however, present financial statements in a different currency.

Indian GAAP

Schedule VI to the Companies Act, 1956 specifies Indian Rupees as the reporting currency.

Statement of Changes in Shareholders' Equity

IFRS

Statement showing capital transactions with owners, the movement in accumulated profit and a reconciliation of all other components of equity. The statement must be presented as a primary statement.

Indian GAAP

Changes in shareholders' equity are disclosed by way of a schedule.

Statement of Recognised Gains and Losses/Other Comprehensive Income

IFRS

Give a statement of recognised gains and losses either as a separate primary statement or highlight it separately in the primary statement of changes in shareholder's equity.

Indian GAAP

Not prescribed

Investments

IFRS

Depends on the classification of investment—if held to maturity or loan or receivable, then carry at amortised cost, otherwise at fair value. Unrealised gains/losses on fair value through profit or loss classification (including trading securities) recognised in the income statement and on available-for-sale investments recognised in equity.**

Indian GAAP

Carry long-term investments at cost (with provision for other than temporary diminution in value). Current investments carried at lower of cost or fair value determined on individual basis or by category of investment but not on overall (or global) basis. Specific guidance exists for banking industry.

** There is an option in IFRS to classify any financial asset 'at fair value through profit or loss'. Changes in fair values in respect of such securities are recognized in the income statement. It must be noted that it is an irrevocable option to classify a financial asset at fair value through profit or loss.

Derivatives and other Financial Instruments — Measurement of Derivative Instruments and Hedging Activities

IFRS

Measure derivatives and hedge instrument at fair value. Recognise the changes in fair value in the income statement, except for effective cash flow hedges, where the changes are deferred in equity until effect of the underlying transaction is recognised in the income statement.

Gains/losses on hedge instrument used to hedge forecast transaction, included in the cost of asset/liability (basis adjustment).

Indian GAAP

No comprehensive guidelines currently. Accounting treatment for forward contracts and equity index and equity stock futures and option is prescribed. Guidance prescribed for banking companies.

Table 6.1 Accounting Differences of IFRS and Indian GAAP

Subject	IFRS	Indian GAAP
Special purposes entities (SPEs)	Consolidate where the substance of the relation ship indicates control.	No specific guidance
Business combinations	All business combinations are acquistions	No comprehensive accounting standard on business combinations. All business combinations are acquisition; however, required use of pooling of interests method in certain amalgam ations [when all the specified conditions are met]. To summarize: On consolidation for an entity acquired and held as an investment: treated as acquisition. On amalgamation of an entity, either uniting of interests or acquisition. On business a cquisition (*i.e.* assets and liabilities only) treated as acquisition.
Uniting of interests method	Prohibited.	Required for certain amalgamations when all the specified conditions are met, else accounted under the purchase method.
Acquired intangible assets	Capitalise if recognition criteria are met; intangible assets must be amortised over useful life. Intangibles assigned an indefinite useful life must not be amorised but reviewed annually for impairment. Revaluations are Revaluations circumstances.	Capitalise if recognition criteria are met; intangible assets must be amortised over useful life with a rebuttable presumption of not excee ding 10 years. Revlaluations not permitted.

Contd..

Subject	IFRS	Indian GAAP
Property, plant and equipment	Use historical cost or revalued amounts. Regular valuations of entire classes of assets are required when revaluation option is chosen.	Use historical cost Revaluations are permitted, however, no requirement on frequency of revaluation. On revaluation, an entire class of assets is revalued, or selection of assets is made on a systematic basis.
Depreciation	Allocated on a systematic basis to each accounting period over the useful life of the asset.	Similar to IFRS, except where the useful life is shorter than that envisaged under the Companies Act or the relevant statute, the depreciation is computed by applying a higher rate.
Deferred income taxes	Use full provision method (some exceptions) driven by balance sheet temporary differences. Recognise deferred tax assets if recovery is probable.	Recognise tax effect of timing difference as deferred tax asset or liability. Recognise deferred tax assets *(a)* for entities with tax losses carry forward, if realisation is virtually certain, whereas *(b)* for entities with no tax losses carry forward, if realisation is reasonably certain. A number of other specific differences.
Fringe benefits tax	Included as part of related expense (fringe benefit) which gives rise to incurrence of the tax.	Disclosed as a separate item after profit before tax on the face of the income statement.
Convertible debt	Account for convertible debt on split basis, allocating proceeds between equity and debt	Convertible debt is recognised as a liability based on legal form without any split.
Functional currency	Currency of primary economic environment in which entity operates.	Does not define functional currency.
Compensated absences	Provision on actual cost to the company basis	Provision based on actuarial valuation

Contd..

Subject	IFRS	Indian GAAP
Preliminary expenses	Charged to income statement.	Deferred and written off over the period of 5 years.
loans Origination Cost	Origination cost is amortized	Charged to Profit and loss account
Financial liabilities - classification	Mandatory redeemable preference shares are classified as liabilities.	All preference shares are classified as shareholders' funds.
Employee benefits - pension costs defined benefit plans	Must use the projected unit credit method to determine benefit obligation	Provision in the accounts is normally made on the basis of actuarial valuation – no specific method is prescribed
Depreciation	Allocated on a systematic basis to each accounting period over the useful life of the asset.	Depreciation is provided based on the useful lives of assets or the minimum rates prescribed by the Indian Companies Act, whichever is higher. Asset lives are not prescribed by the Companies Act, but can be derived from the depreciation rates.
Capitalisation of borrowing costs	Permitted, but not required for qualifying assets.	Compulsory when relates to the construction of certain assets.
Foreign exchange fluctuation	Under IAS such gains or losses are required to be expensed	Indian GAAP requires that any profit/loss arising on the restatement of foreign exchange liabilities incurred for the acquisition of imported fixed assets as a result of change in exchange rates is change as part of the original cost of the assets.
Impairment of long lived assets	IAS require that assets be reviewed for impairment and impairment losses recognized in the accounts	Indian GAAP also has adopted the provisions of IFRS with effect from 1.4 2004 for listed companies and commercial enterprise with a turnover > 50 crores

Contd..

Subject	IFRS	Indian GAAP
Leasehold land	Disclosed as prepaid assets and accounting treatment is similar to operating leases.	Disclosed as a part of fixed assets.
Changes in accounting policies	Restate comparatives andprior-year opening retained earnings.	Include effect in the income statement of the period in which the change is made except as specified in certain standards where the change resulting from adoption of the standard has to be adjusted against opening retained earnings.
Correction of fundamental errors	Restatement of comparatives is mandatory.	Include effect in the current year income statement with appropriate disclosure
Deferred taxes	Use full provision method (some exceptions), driven by balance sheet temporary differences. Recognise deferred tax assets if recovery is probable.	Deferred tax assets and liabilities should be recognised for all timing differences subject to consideration of prudence in respect of deferred tax assets.
Lease Accounting	Has been in place for a much longer time.	Applicable since 2001
Asset Retirement Obligation (ARO)	Obligations that are legally enforceable and unavoidable, and are associated with the retirement of tangible long-lived assets, be recorded as liabilities when those obligations are incurred and recorded at fair value.	No such guidance available.

Source: www.nirc-icai.org/backgroundmaterial/a109.ppt

General Differences

- IFRS provides much less overall detail than GAAP
- IFRS contains relatively little industry-specific instructions as compared to GAAP.
- IFRS use a single-step method for impairment write-downs rather than the two-step method used in U.S. GAAP
- IFRS does not permit Last In First Out (LIFO) as inventory costing method.
- IFRS has a different probability threshold and measurement objective for contingencies.
- IFRS does not permit curing debt covenant violations after year-end.

Challenges Involved in Adoption of IFRS and Implementation Issues

1. *IFRS Hierarchy International Accounting Standards Committee Foundation*: The body which oversees the International Accounting Standards Board. International Accounting Standards Board (IASB) — The body which sets International Financial Reporting Standards (IFRS) and approve interpretations International Financial Reporting Interpretations Committee (IFRIC) — Responsible for interpretation of standards and issue guidance on issues that have not yet been addressed by standards. The Standards Advisory Council (SAC)— Forum to provide broad strategic advice on IASB's agenda priorities and insight into costs and benefits of projects.
2. IFRS Hierarchy Statements IFRS are as principles based set of standards that establish broad rules and also dictate specific treatments. International Financial Reporting Standards comprises of International Accounting Standards (IAS) International Financial Reporting Standards (IFRS) Standard Interpretations (SIC) International Financial Reporting Interpretations (IFRIC).
3. Convergence to IFRS Globally More than 100 countries throughout the world, including the 27 European Union

member states, require or permit the use of International Financial Reporting Standards (IFRS), developed by the IASB. The number of countries adopting IFRS is expected to increase to 150 by the end of 2011. Countries such as China and Canada have announced their intention to adopt IFRS from 2008 and 2011 respectively.

4. Convergence to IFRS Globally by 2011, it is expected that:
   - All major countries will have adopted IFRS to some extent
   - China and Japan will be substantially converged to IFRS
   - US public companies will likely have the option of using either IFRS of US GAAP
   - Substantial majority of Global Fortune 500 will report under IFRS

   The SEC has issued a roadmap whereby a few big US corporations would begin reporting according to IFRS by 2014. Full conversion would be done by 2016 depending upon the size of the entity.

5. IFRS Roadmap in India Phase 1 Phase 2 Phase 3 Date Opening Balance sheet Opening Balance sheet Opening Balance sheet as of April 1, 2011 as of April 1, 2013 as of April 1, 2013 Coverage I) Companies which are part Companies not covered in Listed companies not covered of NSE Index – Nifty 50 phase 1 and having net worth in the earlier phases exceeding INR 500 Crore II) Companies which are part of BSE Sensex – BSE 30 Companies whose shares or other securities are listed on a stock exchange outside India Companies, whether listed or not, having net worth of more than INR1,000 Crore. If the financial year of a company commences at a date other than 1 April, then it shall prepare its opening balance sheet If the financial year of a company commences at a date other than 1 April, then it shall prepare its opening balance sheet at the commencement of immediately following financial year. at the commencement of immediately following financial year.

6. Fair Value Measurement IFRS requires application of fair value in various situations and this would result in significant difference from currently presented financial information. This would increase the volatility in reported earnings and related performance measures such as EPS, P/E ratio, etc. There may be interpretation issues of IFRS among businesses and accounting bodies. Various adjustments to the fair value may result in gains or losses which are reflected in the income statements. Whether this can be included in computing distributable profit. This needs further debate and clarification.
7. *Fair Value Measurement:* For instance, real estate companies would have to take a relook at their construction agreements for the purposes of revenue recognition. Under IFRS, a company would be able to recognizes revenue with reference to stage of completion, if and only if, the agreement transfers control to the buyer, as well as the significant risks and rewards of the ownership of the work. Further, accurate information on the fair value of the transaction may not always be easy to get or may depend on the availability of related professional.
8. *Amendments in Regulations Accounting Standard:* Are not only issued by The Institute of Chartered Accountants of India (ICAI) but also issued by but also by various other regulatory bodies, such as The Securities and Exchange Board of India (SEBI), The Reserve Bank of India (RBI) and The Insurance Regulatory and Development Authority (IRDA) and National Advisory Committee on Accounting Standards (NACAS) established by the Ministry of Corporate Affairs. There is a critical need that all such regulatory bodies need to be consistent.
9. *Amendments in Regulations Companies Act:* prescribes the requirement of compliance with accounting standards issued by ICAI. Schedule VI of the companies Act defines the format of financial and reporting structures however whereas the presentation requirements are significantly different under

IFRS. Under IFRS, expenses can be classified by nature (salary, rent, power and fuel) or by function (cost of revenues, selling expenses, general and administrative). Schedule VI requires classification by nature.

10. *Amendments in Regulations Income Tax Act*: Computation of taxable income is governed by detailed provisions of the Indian Income Tax Act, 1961. Convergence with IFRS will require significant changes/clarifications from the tax authorities on treatment of various accounting transactions. For example, consider unrealized losses and gains derivatives that are required to be marked under IFRS. Different taxation frameworks may possible for the tax treatment of such unrealized gains and losses.

11. *Amendments in Regulations Regulatory Guidelines:* RBI and IRDA regulate the financial reporting for banks, financial institutions and insurance companies, respectively, including the presentation format and accounting treatment for certain types of transactions. Several of these guidelines currently are not consistent with the requirements of IFRS.

12. *Amendments in Regulations Regulatory Guidelines:* The SEBI has also prescribed guidelines for listed companies with respect to presentation formats for quarterly and annual results and accounting for certain transactions, some of which are not in accordance with IFRS. For example, Clause 41 of the Listing Agreement allows companies to publish and report only standalone quarterly financial results, however IFRS considers only consolidated financial statements as the primary financial statements for reporting purpose.

13. *Amendments in Regulations Court procedures:* Apex courts in India approve accounting under amalgamation/restructuring schemes, which may not be in accordance with the accounting principles/standards. Under the current accounting/legal framework such legally approved deviations from the accounting standards are acceptable. Such approved deviations may not be in line with the IFRS.

14. IT System Changes Conversion to IFRS will require extensive upgrades or total replacement of major system. Various ERP applications, to be enhanced, upgraded or replaced. For example, ERP modules such as inventory (IFRS does not LIFO method), asset management (Depreciation accounting and asset valuation), reporting (three years of comparative financial information) project accounting and purchasing may require configuration modifications, and every modification to an application may affect others.
15. IT System Changes Certain IT applications other than ERP may require changes such as software for management reporting, regulatory compliances, financial analytics, etc. It is likely that new GL accounts will have to be established and embedded appropriately in upstream and downstream systems or related ERP sub-modules.
16. Determine the Impact Due to the significant differences between Indian GAAP and IFRS, adoption of IFRS is likely to have a significant impact on the financial position and financial performance of most Indian companies. Major are which will impact are inventory, asset management, taxation including deferred tax, financial reporting, project accounting and purchasing, etc.
17. Determine the Impact Conversion from Indian accounting standards with IFRS will have an impact on some fundamental accounting practices followed in India as mentioned below: Fair value concept, Substance over form, Financial disclosures, Restatement of financial statements, Determination of functional currency, and other aspects.
18. Determine the Impact Most aspects of the business can be The adoption of IFRS affects more than a company's accounting policies, processes, and people. Ultimately, most aspects of a company's business and operations are affected: affected potentially. Processes and systems Operations Tax Treasury Examples include impact on: Debt covenants Compensation plans Revenue contracts Joint ventures and alliances Investor communication Source: ASSOCHAM Master Class on IFRS.

19. *Determine the Impact Financial Disclosures*: Financials are disclosed in line with Schedule V1 of Companies Act and which differs that IFRS. IFRS is more focused on qualitative information for the stakeholders such as terms of related party transactions, risk management policies, currency exposure for the entity with sensitivity analysis, etc. Schedule V1 emphasized more on quantitative information such as sales quantity, amount of transaction with related parties, production capacities, CIF value of imports and income and expenditure in foreign currency, etc.

20. D*etermine the Impact Restatement of Financial Statements*: Financials are disclosed in line with Schedule V1 of Companies Act and which differs that IFRS. IFRS is more focussed on qualitative information for the stakeholders such as terms of related party transactions, risk management policies, currency exposure for the entity with sensitivity analysis, etc. Schedule V1 emphasized more on quantitative information such as sales quantity, amount of transaction with related parties, production capacities, CIF value of imports and income and expenditure in foreign currency, etc.

21. *Determine the Impact Determination of Functional Currency*: India entities prepare their financial statements in Indian rupees. However, under IFRS, entities need to measures its assets, liabilities, revenues and expenses in its functional currency. Functional currency is the currency that best reflects the economic substance of the underlying events and circumstances relevant to the entity.

22. *Determine the Impact Other Aspects*: Preference share capital of company is reported as part of the shareholder's fund. However, IFRS does not consider it as part of shareholder's fund. Hence, it may significantly impact the net worth of companies that have issued preference shares. India entities prepare their financial statements in Indian rupees. Such companies may get into a situation after implementing IFRS that their net worth either may significantly reduced or get negative. India GAAP requires provisions for proposed

dividend even declared after the balance sheet date. IFRS Under IFRS, liability of dividends is recorded in the period in which it is declared.

23. *Determine the Impact Other Aspects*: Under India GAAP, all intangible assets have a definite life, which cannot generally exceed 10 years. Under IFRS, certain intangible assets may have indefinite lives and useful lives in excess of 10 years. IFRS permit interest paid to be disclosed either as financing cash flows or as operating cash flows. The Indian standards require that interest paid be reflected as a financing cash flow only.

24. *Convert Historical Data Convert Historical Data*: Historical data from recent prior periods will have to be recast for comparative purposes. This is necessary to permit accurate and comparative trend and ratio analysis. Record retention requirements should be reviewed to ensure that data currently being retained is detailed enough to permit proper restatement of prior-period financials. The degree of complexity likely to be faced will depend on many different factors and will be influenced by issues such as the number of countries the business operates in, the current state of financial reporting systems and processes, technical accounting matters and the availability of internal resources with the appropriate technical skills.

25. *Availability of Professionals:* There is a lack of adequate professionals with practical IFRS conversion experience and therefore many companies will have to rely on external advisers and their auditors. Training to internal staff is critical for successful transition. A core group of internal staff (the project team) will also be needed to work on the conversion process. Depending on the size of the programme, some staff may be required on a full-time basis.

26. SMEs face problems in implementing IFRSs because of:

    i. Scarcity of resources and expertise with the SMEs to achieve compliance;

ii. Cost of compliance not commensurate with the expected benefits.

27. Training to Preparers:

i. Some IFRS are complex;

ii. There is lack of adequate skills amongst the preparers and users of Financial Statements to apply IFRSs;

iii Proper implementation of such IFRSs requires extensive education of preparers.

28. Interpretation:

i. A large number of application issues arise while applying IFRSs;

ii. There is a need to have a forum which may address the application issues in specific cases.

Conclusion

Irrespective of the various challenges, adoption of IFRSs in India will significantly change the contents of corporate financial statements as a result of:

- More refined measurement of performance and state of affairs;
- Enhanced disclosures leading to greater transparency.

With rapid liberalization process experienced in India over the past decade, there is now a huge presence of multinational enterprises in the country. Furthermore, Indian companies are also investing in foreign markets. This has generated an interest in Indian GAAPs by all concerned. In this context, the role of Indian accounting standards, which are becoming closure to IFRSs, has assumed a greater significance from the point of view of global financial reporting.

Indian companies using the Indian accounting standards are experiencing fewer difficulties accessing international financial markets, are Indian accounting standards are becoming closer to the IFRSs. Indian standards are expected to converge even further in the future, especially after the challenges mentioned in study are addressed over the next few years.

REFERENCES

1. International Accounting Standards Board (2007), International Financial Reporting Standards 2007 (including International Accounting Standards (IAS(tm)) and Interpretations as at 1 January 2007), LexisNexis, ISBN 1-4224-1813-8.
2. Original Texts of IAS/IFRS, SIC and IFRI C adopted by the Commission of the European Communities and Published in Official Journal of the European Union http://ec.europa.eu/internal_market/accounting/ias_en.htm#adopted-commission.
3. Case Studies of IFRS Implementation in Brazil, Germany, India, Jamaica, Kenya, Pakistan, South Africa and Turkey, Prepared by the United Nations Intergovernmental Working Group of Experts on International Standards of Accounting and Reporting (ISAR).
4. Ramesh.P.R and Haskins Deloitte (2008) "Convergence with IFRS—Challenges and Strategies".
5. Batra Yash, Challenges in Convergence of India GAAP to IFRS.
6. AICPA Backgrounder, "International Financial Reporting Standards (IFRS)", www.ifrs.com/updates/aicpa/Backgrounder_pdf.html
7. KPMG (2006), "International Financial Reporting Standards-views on a Financial Reporting Revolution", http://us.kpmg.com/microsite/FSLibraryDotCom/docs/IFRS_financial_reporting_revolution.pdf
8. Centre on Transnational Corporations United Nations), United Nations , "International Accounting and Reporting Issues",.
9. Wiley Guide to Fair Value Under IFRS [6], John Wiley & Sons.
10. Accounting at the Open Directory Project.
11. The International Accounting Standards Board—Free access to all IFRS Standards, News and Status of Projects in Progress.
12. Price Water House Coopers Taiwan IFRS Center.
13. The Latest IFRS News and Resources from the Institute of Chartered Accountants in England and Wales (ICAEW).
14. Initial Publication of the International Accounting Standards in the Official Journal of the European Union PB L 261 13-10-2003.
15. Ernst & Young Newsletters, Regulatory Updates, Web-based Learning
16. IAS Plus — Comprehensive site on IFRS, Maintained by Deloitte.
17. Free 2010 IFRS Pocket Guide from IASPlus — Deloitte.

18. Deloitte: An Overview of International Financial Reporting Standards.
19. KPMG IFRS Group with News and Downloadable Documents.
20. The American Institute of CPAs (AICPA) in Partnership with its Marketing and Technology Subsidiary, CPA 2 Biz, has Developed the IFRS.com web site.
21. U.S. Securities and Exchange Commission Proposal for First-time Application of International Financial Reporting Standards by Foreign Private Issuers Registered with the SEC.
22. Accounting Standards.
23. Financial Reporting Solutions Financial Reporting is a Critical Process Involving the Collection, Analysis, Summarization, and Presentation of the Financial Performance of a Business.
24. IFRS for SMEs Presented by Michael Wells, Director of the IFRS Education Initiative at the IASC Foundation.
25. ACCA Approved IFRS Training Firm presented by PIRON Education Pvt. Ltd. Retrieved from "http:// en.wikipedia.org/ wiki/ International Financial Reporting Standards".
26. www.aicpa.org
27. www.ifrs.com
28. www.nirc-icai.org/backgroundmaterial/a109.ppt
29. www.ifrs.com/updates/aicpa/Backgrounder_pdf.html

International Accounting Standards and India's Preparedness

Prof. Radhakrishna Mishra

ABSTRACT

The Ministry of Corporate Affairs, Government of India has declared that IFRS to be implemented in India from 1st April 2011. This decision is purely based on the two facts: Globalization of economies calls for uniformity in accounts throughout the world and Foreign Direct Investors will give more weightage to those countries where IFRS is followed. The declaration has caused a dilemmatic situation and has put a question mark on its successful application by the Indian accounting firms. Though the Indian Accounting Standards are formed in line with International Accounting standards but there are some differences which can affect the financial health of the corporate houses if IFRS is directly implemented to Indian business houses. That is the reason the Indian Accounting Standard Committee is planning to harmonize the Indian Accounting Standards in line with IFRS.

Introduction

Accounting Standards are set of rules and regulations generally followed that help to ensure a common basis for financial statements of different organizations. This means that people can understand these statements more easily and make useful comparisons. Accounting bodies throughout the world have tried to achieve some uniformity in the accounting policies by prescribing accounting standards in orders to narrow the range of alternatives available to an organization in respect of collection and presentation of accounting information.

Accounting information includes Financial Statements that are major source of information influencing the key decisions made by the top authorities of the corporate houses, the investors and other users of accounting information. The US is the leader in financial reporting, and the US Securities and Exchange commission is respected for its role in formulating and implementing US GAAP despite the general vote of confidence. In India, the statements on Accounting Standards are issued by the Institute of Chartered Accountants of India (ICAI) to establish standards that have to be compiled with to ensure that financial statements are prepared in accordance with generally accepted accounting standards in India (Indian GAAP).

International Accounting Standards committee (IASC) is established in 1973 to formulate the accounting standards, (now is known as IFRS Foundation). These standards are created by industrialized nations to provide a world-wide acceptable set of rules that could harmonize the procedure of financial reporting throughout the world.

The Objective of the Committee

The committee is having the following two broad objectives:

- To formulate, publish and promote the use of accounting standards worldwide; and
- To work for the improvement and harmonization of regulations, accounting standards and procedures relating to financial statements.

The IFRS have assumed great importance in recent times because of:

i. Globalization of the economies has led the companies to expand their operations across the borders and this calls for uniformity in accounts of units located in different countries;

ii. Foreign investors would give more weight age to the accounts of those companies which are based on International Financial Reporting Standards.

Adaptability of IFRS

Many countries have adopted IFRS. In 2005, the European Union began requiring companies incorporated in its member states whose securities are listed on an EU-regulated stock exchange to prepare their consolidated financial statements in accordance with IFRS. Australia, New Zealand and Israel have essentially adopted IFRS as their national standards. Canada, which previously planned convergence with US GAAP, now plans to require IFRS for publicly accountable entities in 2011. The Accounting Standards Board of Japan (ASBJ) and the International Accounting Standards Board (IASB) plan convergence by 2011. In India, the ministry of corporate affairs has prepared a roadmap for its implementation as per which BSE 30 and Nifty 50 companies as well as those with shares listed overseas and those with a net worth of over Rs. 1,000 crore have to implement the IFRS by April 1, 2011. Companies with a net worth of more than Rs. 500 crore and less than Rs. 1,000 crore have time till April 1, 2013 while by April 1, 2014, all companies whether listed or not and with a net worth of less than Rs. 500 crore will have to switch over to the new accounting standards.

In a survey conducted by International Federation of Accountants (IFAC), a large chunk of accounting leaders from around the world agreed that a single set of International Standards is important for economic growth. AICPA Chairman Randy Fletchall, CPA and AICPA president and CEO Barry Melancon, CPA, were among those surveyed. Of the 143 leaders from 91 countries who responded, 90 per cent reported that a single set of international financial reporting standards was 'very important' or 'important' for economic growth in their countries.

IFAC survey with respect to the importance of convergence to International Financial Reporting Standards for economic growth in their countries:

- 55 per cent of respondents said IFRS adoption was 'very important' to economic growth
- per cent said 'important'
- per cent 'somewhat important'
- 1 per cent 'not important'

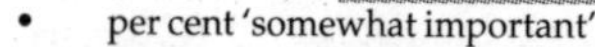

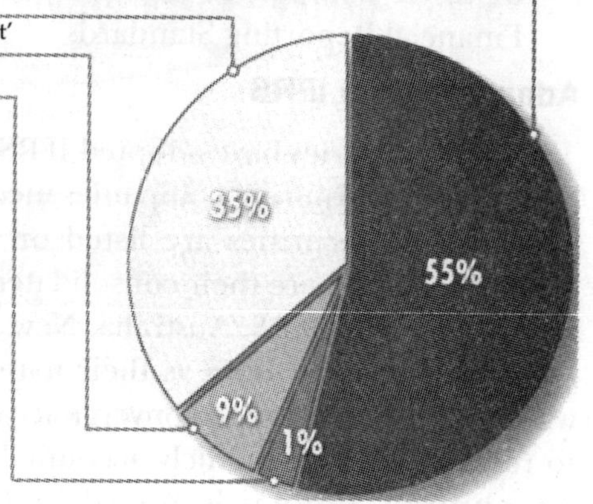

(source: http://ifac.org/globalsurvey)

Comparison of CG Norms in India with Other Countries

Indian Companies listed in stock exchanges abroad have to prepare accounts with respect to GAAP followed in respective countries. Foreign companies having subsidiaries in India have to prepare their accounts in order to meet overseas reporting. FDI and FIIs are more comfortable with one global accounting language which can be understood globally.

Currently IFRS has been made applicable from the reporting year 2011 (or 2011-12, as the case may be) by Ministry of Corporate Affairs for the following:

- Listed companies;
- Bank, Insurance companies, Mutual funds and Financial Institutions;
- Turnover in preceding year exceed Rs. 1 Billion;
- Borrowing in preceding year exceed Rs. 250 Million.

India's shift to the International Financial Reporting Standards (IFRS) could lead to chaos if the government fails to clarify on areas such as net worth requirements, comparative numbers and the calculation of income-tax.

For the effective implementation of IFRS the Institute of Chartered Accountants of India has made certain modifications with the existing accounting standards prevailing in India:

The following standards are not considered in Indian context:

S. No.	International Financial Reporting Standard		
	No.	Title of the Standard	Reasons
1.	IAS 29	Financial Reporting in Hyper-inflationary Economies	Hyper-inflationary conditions do not prevail in India. Accordingly, the subject is not considered relevant in he Indian context.
2.	IFRS1	First-time Adoption of International Financial Reporting Standards	In India, Indian ASs are being adopted since last many years and IFRSs are not being adopted for the first time Therefore, the IFRS 1 is not relevant to India at present

Accounting Standards presently under preparation corresponding to the International Financial Reporting Standards

S. No.	International Financial Reporting Standards		Status of the corresponding Indian Standard
	No.	Title of the Standard	
1.	IAS 26	Accounting and Reporting by Retirement Benefit Plans	Under Preparation.
2.	IAS 32	Financial Instruments: Presentation	• Note ICAI has already issued AS 31 which is mandatory w.e.f. April 1, 2011. Differences due to legal and regulatory environment • The Exposure Draft of proposed Standard does not deal with certain aspects which are not permitted under the present Indian

(Contd...)

			legal framework for example, derivatives based on an enterprise's own equity instruments and buy back of shares by the enterprise itself for issuance to employees under ESOPs. • As per IAS 32, redeemable preference shares, based on their substance, may be considered as a debt instrument instead of equity instrument. In Indian legal framework, the settled position is to consider these as part of equity ICAI has decided to retain IAS 32 position in the Exposure Draft of proposed Indian Accounting Standard. However, it is recognised in the Exposure Draft itself that until the law is amended, the law will prevail over the Standard.
3.	IAS 39	Financial Instruments: Recognition and Measurement	Note ICAI has already issued AS 30 which is mandatory w.e.f. April 1, 2011. There are no major differences compared to IAS 39.
4.	IAS 41	Agriculture	Under preparation.
5.	IFRS 2	Share-based Payment	At present, Employee share Based Payments, are covered by a Guidance Note issued, by by the ICAI which is based on IFRS 2 insofar as fair value approach is concerned It, allows adoption of intrinsic value however, method unitl the formulation of the

(Contd...)

			Standard Further, some other pronouncements deal with other share-based payments, *e.g.*, AS 10, Accounting for Fixed Assets.
6.	IFRS 4	Insurance Contracts	Under preparation.
7.	IFRS 7	Financial Instruments: Disclosures	Note ICAI has already issued AS 32 which is mandatory w.e.f. April 1, 2011.

Guidance Note issued by the Institute of Chartered Accountants of India (ICAI) corresponding to the International Financial Reporting Standard

S.No	International Financial Reporting Standard		Title of the Guidance Note
	No.	Title of the Standard	Guidance Note on Accountingand
1.	IFRS 6	Exploration for and Evaluation of Mineral Resources	for Oil and Gas Producing Activities. The Guidance Note is comprehensive as it deals with all accounting aspects is based on the corresponding US GAAPs

(http://wircicai.org/WIRC_REFERENCER/Acconting%20&%20Auditing/Comparison%20of%20IFRS%20and%20Indian%20Accounting%20Standards.htm#_ftnref1)

Challenges of IFRS

The impact of IFRS exists for companies such as presentation of accounts, accounting policies and procedures, language of legal document, the way the entity will look at its business model and conduct business. At the transition state itself company has to give careful thought and planning for its accounting policy and procedure because it in turn will affect the financial position of company and its operations. It is better for the Indian companies to have a early start of the implementation of IFRS and come up with IFRS roadmap because Government is not looking forward to extend the date of 2011.

In India, at least 16 firms, including Infosys, Wipro and Tata Motors already publish their accounts in this format while 400 companies are working on this. Among the early converts will be IT companies since their operations are more aligned with global standards. Ultimately it will be the obligation of the management to comply with the requirements and the auditors will only have to comment on whether the management has properly compiled with or not.

Though the corporate houses are bracing up to converge with International Financial Reporting Standards from April 1, 2011 but there are dissenting voices with the government departments regarding its hasty implementation. It is difficult to implement IFRS from April next year because the National Advisory Committee on Accounting Standards (NACAS) has still not notified the IFRS—compliant accounting standards (AS). The time NACAS notified is too little. Simultaneously, the stakeholders' education is another issue yet to be accomplished.

This may impact the companies from the point of view of tax implications as the IFRS mandates marking assets to market and India's income tax act calculates tax on the basis of real income. Mark to market means assessing an asset on fair value. This is the biggest challenge in implementing IFRS. This may impact the 300-odd companies which are likely to converge to the IFRS beginning next fiscal.

Apart from the above issues another vital part of the challenge needs high attention the lack of trained manpower in IFRS. For that purpose a number of front line audit firms have tied up with different institutions to train their employees.

Managing IFRS Conversion

According to the Institute of Chartered Accountants of India (ICAI), it is the finance ministry that has to clarify the matter and amend I-T Act for the purpose. However, finance ministry officials are of the view that world-wide two separate accounts are maintained by companies—one is for tax purposes and the other is IFRS-compliant for disclosures. Therefore, there are no tax implications as such and the Indian companies can also prepare two sets of accounts. The finance ministry is planning to take up the issue with the corporate affairs ministry.

In fact, the officials claimed, maintaining two sets of accounts would help in avoiding confusion as the IFRS is important mainly for disclosures.

It is to be noted that the US and Japan have still not committed towards the adoption or convergence with the IFRS. For the income tax purpose, all subsidiaries of a group have to be assessed individually and not as a group. However, IFRS prefers a consolidated statement of the group and not of subsidiaries. This fundamental difference will create huge confusion for corporate houses and more so for shareholders.

Conclusion

Rather than transition we should follow convergence and the ICAI also trying to do the same. Under this approach the Indian accounting standards are modified to fit to the IFRS. This can solve the problem of discrepancy that will arise if we directly follow IFRS. If IFRS is completely adopted in India most of the companies' financial statements will show lower profits than what would have been under Indian GAAP. There may be the question in mind of layman stakeholders that how can the profits of a company change drastically by following different GAAP but this is not necessarily due to a 'faulty' reporting system adopted by the companies but because of inherent IFRS-GAAP differences. (Notable differences exist in IFRS fixed assets and IFRS inventory standards.)

REFERENCES

1. Financial Accounting, ICFAI Publication, ISBN No. – 81-7881-624-5
2. The Business World — 16th July 2010.
3. www.moneybol.com
4. www.icai.org
5. www.ifac.org
6. www.cfoinnovation.com

Why Consistency of Accounting Standards Matters

A Contribution to the Principles VS. Rules Debate in Financial Reporting

Dr. Fisseha Girmay Tessema
Dr. Aravind.S.

ABSTRACT

Currently, the International Accounting Standards Board (IASB) and Financial Accounting Standards Board (FASB) are undertaking a project to develop a common conceptual framework that ...is both complete and internally consistent. Such a framework would provide a sound foundation for developing future accounting standards and is essential to fulfilling the Boards' goal of developing standards that principles-based, internally consistent, internationally converged, and that lead to financial reporting that provides the information needed for investment, credit, and similar decisions. That framework, which will deal with a wide range of issues, will build on the existing IASB and FASB frameworks and consider developments since they issued their original frameworks. An overview of the importance of the Framework, why the existing Framework does not fully meet the needs of the IASB, FASB, and other accounting standard setters, and the need to revisit document are discussed in Bullen and Crook (2005) and Johnson (2004a. b. and 2005). As explained in these IASB and FASB staff papers, several gaps in the Framework need to be fulfilled and a number of areas need to be updated.

A cross-firm consistent application of accounting standards is sought in all major accounting systems. Since many transactions and events are only vaguely or not explicitly addressed in the standards managers must often use judgement when applying accounting standards to particular transactions or events. This analysis concludes that a consistent application of accounting standards can only be ensured if the accounting standards themselves are internally consistent. By contrast, inconsistent standards—in the absence of clear guidance—permit managers to (more or less arbitrarily) choose between different accounting methods. Moreover, it is found that a consistent application presupposes the existence of specific guidance ('rules') in order to frame management's judegment. It is argued that the reliance on principles only—as requested by many in the accounting literature—fails to ensure a consistent application because it allows management to exert judgement differently in identical cases. The assessment includes arguments and propositions from the international discussion in the accounting literature and also refers to other related fields of research, such as legal theory.

Keywords: Conceptual framework; Accounting Choices; Principles *vs.* Rules Debate; Standard Setting.

Introduction

Ever since the occurrence of accounting scandals such as Enron in the beginning of the millennium, the principles *vs.* rules debate has been on top of the agenda of securities regulators, especially of the U.S. Securities and Exchange Commission (SEC), and of national and international standard setters and accountancy bodies, such as the U.S. Financial Accountizng Standards Board (FASB), the International Accounting Standards Board (IASB) and the Institution of Chartered Accountants of India (FASB, 2002, 2004; Tweedie, 2002, 2005, SEC, 2003; ICAI, 2006). The topic has been controversial in national and international journals.

The origins of the discussion go back to the early twentieth century. Until then, practitioners in the U.S. and elsewhere failed to implement uniform accounting standards. They argued that the choice of accounting methods, which appropriately reflect the economic substance of specific transactions and events, requires the use of professional judgment (Previts and Merino, 1998, p. 163). That is, 'the application of relevant knowledge and experience, within the context provided by... accounting standards... in reaching decisions where a choice must be made between alternative possible courses of action' (Mason and Gibbins, 1988). However, with the proliferation of different opinions about the proper accounting methods and the crash of the U.S. stock market in 1929, there was a call for the establishment of uniform accounting standards which would limit management's use of professional judgment and enhance the comparability of financial statements (Previts and Merino, 1998, pp. 161 et seq.).

Since then it has been widely accepted that 'by articulating the best thinking about the issues, accounting standards will produce better financial reporting, at least on the average, than would exist in their absence' (Mason and Gibbins, 1991, p. 21). In the U.S. the call for comparability has, amongst other things, led to what may be called an excessive overregulation. As a consequence of the corporate accounting scandals some of the accounting literature expresses concerns with rules-based accounting and there are increasingly calls for a principles-based approach to standard setting (FASB, 2002, 2004; SEC, 2003).

Another topic that plays a major role in the planned reformation of the world's prevailing accounting systems—IFRS and U.S. GAAP—is the elimination of inconsistencies and thus the quest for internal consistency of the respective systems (IASB, 2008, P4, BC2.46). The accounting literature distinguishes between two notions of consistency: on the one hand internal consistency of accounting standards, and on the other hand consistency in the application of those standards. While internal consistency requires that 'any individual standard adopted should be consistent with the existing system of standards'), consistency in the application 'refers to use of the same accounting policies and procedures, either from period to period within an entity or in a single period across entities' (IASB, 2008, QC16).

Internal consistency as well as application consistency across companies has traditionally been sought in all major accounting systems. Interestingly, the reasons for the pursuit of this objective are quite different in different systems. FASB Concepts Statement No. 2 proposes that the U.S. Conceptual Framework 'is a coherent system of interrelated objectives and fundamentals that is expected to lead to consistent standards' and emphasizes the need for a cross-firm consistent choice of accounting policies by stating that 'the public is naturally skeptical about the reliability of financial reporting if two enterprises account differently for the same economic phenomena' (CON 2.16). It explains the need for consistency in relation to comparability: 'Comparability between enterprises and consistency in the application of methods over time increases the informational value of comparisons of relative economic opportunities or performance' (CON 2.111). In their draft for a revised conceptual framework the FASB and the IASB similarly point out that 'although a single economic phenomenon can be faithfully represented in multiple ways, permitting alternative accounting methods for the same economic phenomenon diminishes comparability and, therefore, may be undesirable' (IASB, 2008, QC19).

One can observe that the different notions of consistency are related in such a way that consistency in the application of accounting standards across companies can only be achieved if the standards are internally consistent. In a system that provides clear rules for each and every accounting issue and in which the application of the rules does not require the use of any judgement, internal consistency between the rules would not be required because consistency in the application across companies would be achieved anyway (AAA FASC, 2003, p. 74). However, such a system does not exist. The continuous issuance of new accounting standards and interpretations in rules-based systems, such as U.S. GAAP reveals that there are always issues not covered by any existing rule as well as rules the application of which requires management to use judgement (Penno, 2008, p. 339). In more principles-based systems, like IFRS, the application of high-level principles to specific accounting issues demands the exertion of judgement in many cases.

In particular judgement is necessary either if a transaction or event is not covered by any accounting standard or if it is only addressed by rather broad principles. In such cases management shall, according to IFRS, develop an accounting policy or interpret the principle by reference to the requirements and guidance in standards dealing with similar and related issues. If the standards addressing similar transactions or events are not consistent with each other, different companies may make different interpretations and choices and thus apply different accounting policies to identical cases. Researchers supporting principles-based accounting standards argue that the restriction of management's judgement that follows from the objective to achieve a consistent application may sometimes impair the relevance of financial reporting information, which they regard to be more important than consistency and comparability (Alexander and Jermakowicz, 2006, p. 150).

Obviously, the rule-versus-principles debate and the discussion on consistency are related. Our article contributes to this debate by addressing two major issues. Initially, the traditional quest for consistency in the application of accounting standards is a given and the analysis considers how the current IFRS system would have to be changed with regard to internal consistency of accounting standards as well as to the relationship between principles and rules in order to achieve consistent application. The emphasis then is on present and possible future IFRS, but U.S.GAAP is relied on also because most of the arguments brought forward in the comprehensive U.S. accounting literature equally apply to IFRS. IFRS and U.S.GAAP are paradigmatic for accounting systems under which the accounting regulation is developed by private standard-setting institutions and do not have immediate legal status.

The second major research question addressed is whether the benefits of principles-based accounting standards, such as an increase in relevance, outweigh the loss of consistency in the application. For this discussion, the previous assumption of consistent application of accounting standards by all companies is relaxed, enabling critical discussion of the advantages and disadvantages of principles-based and rules-based accounting standards. For reasons of comparability, enforceability and objectivity of financial reporting information, it is concluded to be important to have specific (internally consistent) accounting requirements that limit management judgment in the application of accounting standards to ideally only one possible accounting method. We acknowledge, however, that this may, in some situations, lead to an impaired relevance of financial reporting information.

Towards Consistency in Normative Accounting Frameworks

The quest for internal consistency is shown here to have developed in different accounting systems. We conclude that a consistent application of accounting standards does not only presuppose the existence of internal consistency of high-level concepts and principles, but also that the rule maker (and managers in the absence of specific guidance) applies the concepts and principles consistently to all comparable accounting issues. This implies that in an internally consistent accounting system there is, in principle, for each transaction and event only one accounting method that accords to the high-level principles as well as to the specific guidance relating to comparable accounting issues and thus consistently fits into the entire 'system' of norms.

U.S. GAAP, and also IFRS all require the use of judgement in the application of accounting standards/norms. Board members and managers under U.S. GAAP and IFRS are supposed to balance between and apply the general concepts to specific cases according to their personal professional judgement, which may differ from case to case. This implies that for some issues there may be several different accounting methods that are all in compliance with the Framework and between which the Board members or management may hence choose.

Consistent application implies that comparable issues are accounted for in the same way across companies (Schipper, 2003, p. 62). We argue that this can only be achieved if standard setters (and managers in the absence of clear guidance) trade-off between and apply the general concepts, such as relevance and reliability, as well as the general recognition and measurement principles consistently to all comparable cases. In an internally consistent accounting system there can be hence for each accounting issue only one accounting method that accords to the high-level concepts principles as well as to the specific guidance relating to comparable accounting issues.

Impossibility of Consistencies

Alexander and Alexander and Jermakowicz (2006) point out that accounting 'is most certainly not a pure science' and conclude that 'internal consistency, as an absolute, is simply not possible'. In another article Alexander (2006) claims that companies' indifferent countries will apply IFRS inconsistently in identical cases and that the enforcement of accounting regulation must accept this. We agree that accounting is not a 'pure science' (see above) and that absolute consistency of all accounting principles is not achievable. Indisputably, one can also agree with Alexander's assumption that IFRS will never be interpreted and applied fully consistently by all companies. However, as in the case of other ideals, such as justice, equality and freedom, the impossibility of achieving absolute internal consistency does not, from a normative perspective, imply that consistency between accounting norms and their consistent application is not to be desired. Nor does it imply that on a comparative basis there cannot be more consistent and less consistent accounting norms.

The Role of Consistency in the IFRS System

We now turn to exploring how far internal consistency is achieved in the IFRS system. The IASB Framework is shown to contain contradictory objectives and qualitative characteristics as well as conflicting general concepts and principles. As a result, Standards and Interpretations dealing with similar and related issues are partly inconsistent. From this finding one can infer that a consistent application of IFRS is currently not ensured. Finally, the IASB's efforts towards the elimination of the described inconsistencies are presented.

The Qualitative Characteristics 'Relevance' and 'Reliability'

It is clear the IASB strives for consistency of its standards. According to the Preface to International Financial Reporting Standards 'the objective of the Framework is to facilitate the consistent and logical formulation of IFRSs' (Para. 8). Moreover, in their proposal of a revised conceptual framework the FASB and the IASB note that 'internal consistency of accounting standards is desirable and that it should naturally result from developing standards that are consistent with the same conceptual framework' (IASB, 2008, BC2.46). Consistent with the U.S. Conceptual Framework the IASB Framework (1989) points out that the Board members in the standard setting process and managers when developing accounting policies for unregulated issues need to trade-off between qualitative characteristics, especially relevance and reliability (FW.45). However, at present, there is no unanimous agreement on what constitutes relevant and reliable information or on how to trade-off adequately between the two qualitative characteristics (Johnson, 2005, p.1). And more recently, the question of whether such a trade-off should exist has been raised. Whether an accounting method provides relevant information depends, amongst other things, on the objective of financial statements and the underlying explicit or implicit accounting theory. If, as according to Sprouse and Moonitz (1962), the objective of financial statements is to provide information about the financial position and changes in the financial position of an enterprise, information about the enterprise's wealth as indicated by its resources (assets) and obligations (liabilities) is considered as relevant (assets/liabilities view). If, as according to Paton and Littleton (1940: 1965), the objective of financial statements is to provide information about the performance of an enterprise, information about the enterprise's efficiency in obtaining inputs to produce and sell outputs as indicated by net periodic profit is regarded as relevant (revenue/expense view). The differences of the two objectives and the related accounting theories as well as, arguably, the impossibility to pursue both at the same time has been evidenced in the Anglo-American literature on accounting theory since the 1920s and lately Ronen (2008, p. 184–5) are examples in the Anglo-American literature.

The existing IASB Framework contains both opposing and inconsistent objectives (FW.15; IAS 1.7). As a consequence, standards contain recognition and measurement principles that reflect different accounting theories and are thus sometimes inconsistent. The following example illustrates the resulting inconsistencies: The IASB has given priority to the revenue/expense view in the recognition of government grants, since the corresponding income shall be allocated over the periods necessary to match them with the related costs (IAS 20.12. By contrast, in the case of biological assets the IASB has given priority to the assets/liabilities view because income shall be recognized independently from the incurrence of the costs when an increase in wealth (indicated by an increase in the asset's fair value) has taken place (IAS 41.12, 41.26).

Furthermore, the existing IASB Framework does not 'convey the meaning of reliability clear enough to avoid misunderstandings' (IASB, 2008, BC2.11). The IASB (2005a) notes that 'for many [Board members], the meaning seems to be verifiability, for some its precision, for some, it may be faithful representation, for a few perhaps all of those plus neutrality. Among constituents, the differences in meaning are much greater.

In cases where the qualitative characteristics 'Relevance' and 'Reliability' suggest different accounting policies, the IASB in the standard setting process and managers in the development of accounting policies when no IFRS addresses the particular transaction or event, need to trade-off between the two qualitative characteristics (FW.45). The IASB Framework does not provide guidance on how to balance relevance and reliability, but rather requires managers to find an appropriate balance between the characteristics by using their professional judgement (FW.45).

In the absence of legal liability this may be tolerable. Given the threat of different assessments in court this imposes an undesirable risk on management even if assessment and application are done in good faith.

The FASB points out that 'no consensus can be expected about their relative importance in a specific situation because different users have or perceive themselves to have different needs and, therefore, have different preferences' (CON2.45). The diverging opinions about the relative importance of relevance and reliability in the accounting literature confirm this statement. For example, Ernst &Young (2005) regard reliability as 'a necessary precondition that must be met for information to be relevant' (p. 2). By contrast, Chambers (1996) argues in the context of measurement that the qualitative characteristics are mutually exclusive and that a trade-off results in information that is neither relevant nor neutral (reliable) (p. 127).

Joyce *et al.* (1982) evidence the low agreement on the meaning and relative importance of the qualitative characteristics by means of an experiment which they claim results in users choosing different accounting policies in identical situations. According to them, 'this casts doubt on the ability of the qualitative characteristics... to facilitate accounting policy making'. One may conclude from these findings that the qualitative characteristics of relevance and reliability do not enable Board members as well as managers in the absence of clear guidance to consistently exercise their professional judgement in the development and application of accounting policies relating to comparable issues.

The General Definitions, Recognition Criteria and Measurement Concepts

Solomon's (1986, pp. 120–1) and Dopuch and Sunder (1980, pp. 6–7) demonstrate by reference to pension obligations and deferred taxes that the liability definition under U.S. GAAP is too broad to be helpful in choosing between different accounting policies. This criticism also applies to the largely comparable liability definition and other financial statement elements definitions in the IASB Framework (FW.60). For example, according to FW.70 (a) income arises from inflows or increases of assets or decreases of liabilities. However, only some increases of assets, such as increases in the fair value of certain financial instruments (IAS 39.55(a)) and biological assets (IAS 41.26), give rise to income, while others, such as increases in the fair value of available-for-sale financial assets (IAS 39.55(b)) and increases in the carrying amount of property, plant and equipment (IAS 16.39) and intangible assets (IAS38.85) resulting from a revaluation, are credited directly to equity and thus do not give rise to income. The fact that the IASB has more or less arbitrarily drawn the line between unrealized increases in assets that are recognized through profit and loss and unrealized asset increases excluded from income (IASB, 2005a, p. 11) reveals that the income definition in the IASB Framework is too broad to limit (arbitrary) choices in the development of accounting policies, either by the Board or by preparers.

The same can be said about the general recognition criteria in the IASB Framework, the probable inflow of future economic benefits associated with an item and its reliable measurement (FW.83). The IASB Framework does not provide any threshold that must be met for the inflow of economic benefits to be regarded as probable. In view of the vagueness of the probability criterion, it is not surprising that the IASB has set different probability requirements for different accounting issues, as evidenced below for the recognition of revenue from the sale of goods and construction contracts. As regards the reliable measurement criterion, the IASB (2005a) has observed that the 'accounting standards have different (inconsistent?) hurdles for sufficiently reliable measurement and different (inconsistent?) treatments for insufficiently reliable measurement' (p. 11). It follows that the general recognition criteria in the IASB Framework do not provide a suitable basis for the consistent deduction of accounting policies in the absence of an IFRS.

Instead of providing guidance on how to find an appropriate measurement attribute in a specific situation, the IASB Framework only lists several measurement bases that are used in the accounting practice (FW.100) (IASB, 2005d, p. 20). Due to the 'lack of an agreed, coherent measurement theory', inconsistencies in the measurement of financial statement elements exist in several IFRS, such as in IAS 39, which is deemed to 'reflect more or less arbitrary mixed measurement compromises spending resolution of conflicting views on appropriate measurement bases' (IASB,2005d, p. 20). This suggests that the required reference to the Framework's measurement concepts in the absence of an IFRS dealing with a specific issue or with related issues does not adequately guide managers' judgement in the choice of a measurement attribute.

Standards and Interpretations Dealing with Similar and Related Issues

Since the IASB has not applied the IASB Framework's general recognition and measurement principles consistently to similar issues, some IFRS are inconsistent. For example, revenue from the sale of goods shall not be recognized until the seller has transferred the significant risks and rewards of ownership to the buyer (IAS18.14 (a)). This typically occurs with the transfer of legal title or the passing of possession to the buyer (IAS 18.15). If the 'risks and rewards criterion' were also to be applied to construction contracts, revenue would generally have to be recognized when construction is complete. It has been argued that in the case of long-term construction contracts, the 'completed contract method' would not appropriately reflect the enterprise's performance during the periods of construction (Paton and Littleton, 1940: 1965, p. 50; IFRIC, 2006, p. 4). Therefore, the IASB makes an exception from the risks and rewards criterion in the case of construction contracts. If the outcome of the contract is reliably measurable IAS 11.22 requires revenue from construction contracts to be recognized according to the stage of completion of contract activity at each balance sheet date, even if the enterprise has not yet transferred legal title or possession to the customer.

The IASB's Efforts towards the Elimination of Inconsistencies

Having recognized that the objectives, concepts and principles in the existing IASB Framework are partly ambiguous and internally inconsistent, the IASB and the FASB began a joint project on the revision and convergence of their conceptual frameworks in 2004. The objective of the project is to develop a common conceptual framework that is 'sound, comprehensive, and internally consistent' and thus constitutes an adequate foundation for the development of consistent, principles-based accounting standards (Bullen and Crook, 2005, p. 1; IASB, 2008, p. 4). This project is expected to last for many years.

One measure that the Boards plan to undertake in respect of the existence of conflicting objectives and accounting theories is to place greater emphasis on providing information on an enterprise's financial position and thus the assets/liabilities view (Dichev 2008, p. 458; Whittington, 2008, pp. 149–50). According to chapter 1 of the Exposure Draft of an improved Conceptual Framework for Financial Reporting the objective of financial statements shall 'only' be to 'provide information about the liabilities and equity)', that is, its financial position (IASB, 2008, OB6). The draft conceptual framework further states that information about an entity's financial performance is also essential (IASB, 2008, OB18, OB22). However, since the term 'performance' is planned to be defined in terms of changes in the entity's financial position, it appears as if the depiction of an enterprise's performance in the original sense (*e.g.*, according to Paton and Littleton, 1940: 1965) shall no longer be a distinct objective of IFRS financial statements, from which consequential recognition and measurement criteria (such as the stage-of-completion method in IAS 11) are developed (similarly Bonham *et al.*, 2009, p. 141).

Apart from this, the Boards intend to replace the term 'reliability' with the term 'faithful representation' in order to clarify its meaning (IASB, 2008, QC16, BC2.12–BC2.15). While this replacement is only supposed to be a clarification, some argue that the change in the wording also brings about a change in the meaning (Whittington, 2008, p. 146–7; see also Walton, 2006, p. 340; Lennard, 2007, paras 3.22–3.23). The currently required trade-off between relevance and reliability shall be substituted by a flow process (IASB, 2005b, paras 3–4), in which the standard setter or, in the absence of an IFRS, managers should first identify the economic phenomena that are relevant in making economic decisions and then choose the recognition and measurement methods the application of which provides the most relevant information (IASB, 2005c, paras 9–22, 2008, QC12) and then assess whether the chosen accounting method is a sufficiently faithful representation of the respective economic phenomena (IASB, 2008, QC13). Apparently, the draft conceptual framework prioritizes 'relevance' over 'faithful representation' (Whittington, 2008, p. 146; Gebhardt and Dean, 2008, p. 222). That is because one will have to choose the most relevant accounting method if the representation of the item is sufficiently faithful, even if there are other (less) relevant methods that would more faithfully represent the item.

In order to remove existing measurement inconsistencies the IASB is currently undertaking a project on measurement objectives. In line with the SEC's notion that the adoption of principles-based standards will probably lead to an increasing employment of fair value (SEC, 2003, III.I.i.) the IASB tentatively concluded that fair value is the most desirable measurement basis on initial recognition (IASB, 2005d, p. 13). In theory, the adoption of fair value as a single measurement attribute would lead to consistency since 'the fair value of any particular asset or liability is the same for every entity' (Barth, 2006, p. 275; see also Barlev and Haddad, 2007, p. 502; Barth, 2007, p. 11; Bromwich, 2007, p. 57). However, in practice the use of valuation methods in the absence of market prices which require managers to make estimates renders it most unlikely that companies calculate the same values in identical circumstances. This implies that internal consistency of accounting standards, for example as regards measurement, does not automatically guarantee a consistent application of the respective standards. Notably, Benston et al. (2006) argue that standard setters need to provide 'very detailed rules for calculating' fair values (p.173). The April 2009 changes to SFAS 157 Fair Value Measurements confirm this. It is, however, not in line with the current trend in standard setting to move from rules-based to more principles-based accounting standards on the one hand. On the other hand it also needs to be considered that providing rules does not automatically create consistency. For example, IAS 39 provides extensive guidance on how to calculate fair values in the absence of market prices. Nevertheless, a consistent valuation of financial instruments is currently not achieved (Financial Stability Forum, 2008, pp. 28 et seq.).

Clarification of the Meaning of 'Rules' and 'Principles'

The link is now made between the consistency issue and the rules-versus-principles debate in the accounting literature. The definitions and distinctive characteristics of rules and principles are identified based on the legal and accounting literatures. It is concluded that the removal of many deficiencies currently perceived in relation to the rules under U.S. GAAP and IFRS does not require a complete elimination of rules, but could also be achieved by a removal of present inconsistencies. Moreover it is demonstrated that a consistent application accounting standards does not only presuppose internal consistency of the accounting standards, but also the provision of rules in the form of specific recognition and measurement requirements.

The Definition of 'Rules' and 'Principles' in the Accounting Literature

The accounting literature distinguishes between rules and principles by reference to their specificity and the degree of judgement that is required in their application: While the SEC, the Institute o Chartered Accountants of Scotland (ICAS) and most researchers characterize rule as being highly detailed and unambiguously prescribing specific accounting methods (SEC, 2003, I.D.; Kivi *et al.*, 2004, p. 11; ICAS, 2006b, pp. 8, 10; see also Mason and Gibbins, 1991, p. 22), principles are typically described as broad guidelines that, instead of providing detailed implementation guidance, require preparers to exercise judgement in applying the principles to specific transactions and events (Tweedie, 2002, 2005, pp. 33–4, 2007, p. 7; Di Piazza, Jr., 2008, p. 7; Tsakumis *et al.*, 2009, pp. 6–7; see also SEC, 2003, para. I.C.; Psaros, 2007, p. 528).

Tweedie (2002, 2007, p.7) points out that in an accounting system that is based on principles only, many individual transactions and events are not explicitly dealt within any standard. In such cases, managers are supposed to select and apply appropriate accounting policies by exercising professional judgement. Dickey and Scanlon (2006) further note that in a principles-based system enforcing agencies are only allowed to second-guess managers' professional judgement if the selected accounting policies are not in conformity with the high-level principles or if the judgement was not made 'in good faith' (pp. 16–17; see also Ng, 2004, p. 20; Tweedie, 2007, p. 8; Bonham *et al.*, 2009, p. 73). They conclude that 'the principles-based_ approach theoretically permits public companies to have differing accounting judgements within the framework of these broad principles' (Dickey and Scanlon, 2006, p. 13).

We hold that many of the problems related to rules under U.S. GAAP and IFRS, such as scope exceptions and excessive implementation guidance, do not require the elimination of all specific guidance as requested by some in the accounting literature. We argue that they may also be resolved by eliminating the inconsistencies within the respective accounting systems. For example, if IAS 39 would require measurement of all financial instruments by reference to a consistent measurement basis the standard would (automatically) contain much less specific guidance.

Impact of the Level of Detail of Accounting Standards on Consistency in Their Application

As shown above, principles-based standards may, even if internally consistent, be applied differently to identical issues by different companies and thus do not ensure consistency in the application of the accounting standards. That is because principles alone do not provide a sufficient structure to limit managers' judgements in the application of the principles to specific transactions and events. This means that if consistency as regards the application of accounting standards is strived for, rules, which are consistently developed on the basis of the high-level principles, need to be provided.

Foe exposition consider: A revenue recognition principle could be that revenue should be recognized when the inflow of economic benefits is probable. Since it depends on managers' judgement when the inflow of economic benefits is regarded as probable, it may happen that in the case of an identical sales contract one company recognizes revenue at contract conclusion while another company recognizes revenue with the receipt of cash. If consistency in the application of accounting standards shall be ensured consistent rules for different types of revenue-generating transactions need to be provided. A rule for the sale of goods could be that revenue shall be recognized when the good is handed over to the customer and no significant additional obligations remain to be fulfilled (more specific [consistent] guidance for additional obligations, such as warranties, may be provided). Since the risk that the sold product does not conform to the contractually agreed specifications is higher in construction contracts than in sales contracts a consistent revenue recognition rule for construction contracts would require the customer's acceptance of the finished product for revenue to be recognized.

Discussion

The following loosens our previous assumption that a consistent application of accounting standards by all companies is required. The advantages and disadvantages of principles-based and rules-based accounting standards are examined, leading to the conclusion that, for reasons of comparability, enforceability and objectivity of financial reporting information, it is important to have specific (internally consistent) accounting requirements that limit managers' judgments in the application of accounting standards to ideally only one possible accounting method. It is acknowledged, however, that this may, in some situations, lead to an impaired relevance of financial reporting information.

Rules-based Standards Increase the Comparability of Financial Reporting Information

Raz (1972) and others consider rules to lead 'more easily to uniform and predictable application' and thus to create consistency and comparability (p. 841; McBarnet and Whelan, 1991, pp. 848–9; ICAS, 2006b, pp. 10–11). By contrast, principles, according to Dickey and Scanlon (2006), may be applied differently to identical cases across companies due to differences in the use of judgement thereby leading to a lack of comparability and consistency in the application of accounting standards (p. 13).

Its recourse by many over several decades suggests that comparability is a desirable characteristic of financial reporting: Especially in the U.S. accounting literature many authors, such as Schipper (2003), emphasize the need for comparability of financial statements (pp. 62–3). In the 1960s discussion by the 'Golden Age' theorists, including Chambers (1966) and Moonitz (1961), comparability was a major postulate underpinning their ideas. Furthermore, it is demanded and much valued by investors (Choi and McCarthy, 2003, p. 7, referring to a letter issued by the Association for Investment Management and Research in 2000), it is one of the very reasons for the existence of accounting standards (Previts and Merino, 1998, pp. 228–34; Schipper, 2003, p. 62) and it underpins the EU's requirement for listed companies to apply uniform accounting standards in the form of IFRS in their consolidated accounts (Article1 IAS Regulation).

However, cross-firm comparability of financial statements, imply that a company showing high income at the end of the accounting period is economically better off than other companies with a lower income number, is not achievable, not even by means of uniform accounting standards. One reason noted by Alexander and Jermakowicz (2006) is that the application of specific rules may require economically different situations to be accounted for identically and thus create a pseudo-comparability (Alexander and Jermakowicz, 2006, p. 150).

Principles-based Accounting Standards Increase the Relevance of Financial Reporting Information

Apart from the creation of a 'pseudo-comparability' in some cases, rules are criticized for failing to capture the particularities of individual cases (Bratton, 2003, p.1037) and for allowing preparers to 'structure transactions round_ the prescriptions, thereby circumventing the intent and spirit of the standards' (Cunningham,2007, p. 11). Principles, by contrast, are regarded as being hardly susceptible to an evasion of their intended purpose (Broshko and Li, 2006, p.5) and, due to their flexibility and the required use of professional judgement, as having the capacity to give consideration to the particularities of individual cases (Bratton, 2003, p. 1037; Cunningham, 2007, p. 11).

Another reason why many, for example, Alexander and Jermakowicz (2006), argue that principles provide more relevant information than rules is that managers' best know the economic reality and how to account for it (p. 150). Others, for example, Bagnoli and Watts (2005), furthermore highlight the positive influence of the existence of implicit accounting choices on the relevance of financial reporting information by providing evidence that managers' accounting policy choices allow the market to infer managers' private information about the firm's economic situation ('signalling effect') (p.798).

However, downside of the flexibility of principles is, according to Beechy (2005), that managers may not always choose the most relevant accounting method since managers are always biased—even if they do not have fraudulent intentions (p.199). Guenther (2005) attributes this, amongst other things, to the pressure to present good results in the short term, especially when the personal income is bound to the achieved results (pp. 6, 12–13). Rentfro and Hooks (2004) additionally remark that the recent corporate scandals, such as the case of Enron, indicate anecdotally that managers do not always apply accounting standards in good faith (p. 89; for the possibility of abuse of imprecise accounting standards see Clarke and Dean, 1992, 1993, 2007). Principles-based accounting standards are hence criticized for providing increased potential for earnings management (Beechy, 2005, pp. 199–200; Benston *et al.*, 2006, p. 173).

In conformity with this, Ewert and Wagenhofer (2005) find that tighter accounting standards reduce earnings management. However, they also find evidence that tighter accounting standards increase real earnings management, that is, a change in the structure of transactions or events in order to avoid the consequences specified by an accounting standard.

Laux and Leuz (2009, pp. 830-1) provide an example that will illustrates the above stated conflict between the relevance of managers' flexibility and the risk of earnings management: Since the measurement of fair value by reference to market prices is—if contagion effects exist—not appropriate, managers must deviate from market prices and determine fair value by means of valuation models in order to provide relevant information. However, it is often not clear under which circumstances market prices are misleading. Laux and Leuz conclude that 'managers have an information advantage over the gatekeeper (*e.g.*, auditors or the SEC) and, as a result, it is difficult to write FVA standards that provide the flexibility when it is needed and constrain managers' behaviour when it is not needed' (p. 831).

Rules-based Standards Increase the Enforceability of Financial Reporting Standards

Since in the case of rules actors know without ambiguity what to do in order to obey rules, the advantage is seen to be in their contribution to certainty and enforceability (ICAS, 2006b, pp. 10–11). On the other hand principles, due to their vagueness, are regarded to be difficult to enforce and thus to create uncertainty (Cunningham, 2007, p. 11).

As stated above, in the case of principles-based standards enforcing agencies have to accept that there will be circumstances where managers of companies account for identical transactions differently. Consequently, the agencies shall only be allowed to second guess managers' professional judgments if the selected accounting policies are not in conformity with the high-level principles or if the judgments were not made 'in good faith'. But, since principles-based standards allow differing interpretations of the broad principles often it will be—especially in the absence of specific guidance—difficult to judge whether an adopted accounting policy conforms to the principles and whether the judgment was made in good faith (Kivi *et al.*, 2004, p. 12). Some therefore doubt that regulators in litigious environments, such as the U.S., will be willing to accept different applications of the same principles (Taub, 2004). Dickey and Scanlon (2006) observe that in this case, preparers would be exposed to a higher risk of litigation because enforcing agencies may allege violation even if the required professional judegment was exerted in good faith (p. 16).

Rules-based Standards Increase the Enforceability of Financial Reporting Standards

In the accounting literature the quest for consistency as regards the application of accounting principles is mostly premised on the desire to achieve output comparability in the form of financial statements (see, *e.g.*, Schipper, 2003, p. 62). Some believe that there is another equally important reason. Apart from providing decision-useful information, accounting is also frequently used for stewardship/contracting purposes, for instance its use in employment contracts and debt covenants, in order to calculate annual bonuses or to limit future debt levels (Watts and Zimmerman, 1986, p. 196). Those other functions—stewardship and accountability—have a long history (Edwards *et al.*, 2009). Guenther (2005), for example, points out those accounting-based contracts only efficiently balance the interests of the contracting parties if there is agreement on how the relevant accounting numbers are calculated (pp. 5–8). As stated above, principles-based accounting standards some-times permit managers to choose between several different accounting methods. With regard to debt covenants, principles-based standards thus enable managers to circumvent covenant restrictions by (voluntarily) changing to a more favorable accounting method (Healy and Palepu, 1990, p. 97, referring to accounting choice sunder U.S. GAAP). Indeed, many researches, for example, Smith and Warner (1979), have provided sound empirical evidence that managers make use of this flexibility in order to avoid costly violations of the contract.

Watts and Zimmerman (1990) argued that flexibility in the choice of accounting policies increases costs and thus decreases contract efficiency (p. 135). That is because lenders either price-protect themselves against managers' 'creative accounting' or they restrict the number of available accounting methods by using fixed GAAP provisions, which are costly to negotiate and monitor for the lender and costly for the borrower because he needs to prepare an extra set of financial statements for contracting purposes. According to Leftwich (1983) another downside of vague principles from a contracting perspective of financial reporting is that they create uncertainty about the terms of the contract and increase the risk of litigation between the contracting parties (pp. 28–9).

From a contracting perspective of financial reporting, it is essential to restrict managers' judgment in the absence of clear guidance to only one possible accounting method. Principles-based accounting standards have been shown not to ensure this since they often permit managers to choose between different accounting methods. A purported advantage of rules-based accounting standards (not necessarily containing bright-line tests that allow managers to circumvent the rules' purpose) is that they provide clear guidance and, through this, limit managers' ability to influence the relevant accounting numbers. Anyhow, if the rules are not internally consistent, managers may, in the absence of concrete guidance, arbitrarily choose between several even opposing accounting policies. From a contracting perspective, specific accounting standards are therefore only effective if they are internally consistent.

It becomes obvious that when discussing whether rules or principles are favorable the possibility of a trade-off between relevance on the one hand and comparability, enforceability and objectivity on the other hand must be considered. The AAA FASC (p. 74) makes the point by providing an example similar to the following one: A rule prescribing that certain assets shall be depreciated over ten years would most probably be applied consistently by all companies, it would create comparability and it would be easily enforceable. However, the rule does not necessarily provide useful information because it fails to reflect the 'real' decline in the asset's economic value. A principle stating that all assets shall be depreciated according to the decline of their economic value in the respective accounting period may provide more relevant information, but it is unlikely that all companies would make identical estimates with regard to the 'real' economic value of a certain asset, that is, the principle would not be applied consistently to identical events by all companies. Furthermore, the estimation of an asset's economic value opens potential for earnings management and it is difficult to judge whether it was made in good faith and thus should not be second-guessed.

Conclusion and Suggestions

For reasons of comparability, enforceability and objectivity it is particularly important to limit managers' judgements in the application of accounting standards to one possible accounting method and thus to provide for a cross-firm consistent application of accounting standards. According to that analysis, the present IFRS system fails, for a large part, to ensure this. That is because the inconsistencies between the objectives, qualitative characteristics and general recognition and measurement criteria in the IASB Framework as well as between the requirements and guidance in certain Standards and Interpretations permit managers to (somctimes arbitrarily) choose between different accounting policies in the absence of clear guidance. This led to the conclusion that consistency in the application of accounting standards requires at least consistency between the accounting standards themselves.

When exploring the differences of principles-based and rules-based accounting standards we found that internal consistency alone cannot sufficiently ensure a coherent application of accounting standards. That is because principles do not provide a sufficient structure to limit managers' judgement in the application of the principles to specific transactions and events. Thus, accounting systems should be based on principles, but should not consist of principles only. There should be a set of high-level principles from which more concrete accounting rules are consistently derived. Due to the consistency between rules addressing comparable issues managers' flexibility in applying accounting standards would be much more limited than under present U.S. GAAP and IFRS.

A normative analysis of the research question focuses on why consistency of accounting standards matters. Further research is required to test empirically or analytically whether internally consistent accounting rules limit managers' judgments in the application of accounting standards. Further research could work out how such a system could be put into practice and what the content of IFRS would have to be.

Finally, it is important to note that we developed our arguments for internal consistency in a normative way, agreeing with Alexander and Jermakowicz's (2006) objection that the 'absolute' consistency of all accounting principles is not achievable (p. 150). However, just as in the case of other ideals, such as justice, equality and freedom, the impossibility to achieve internal consistency in absolute terms, from a normative perspective, does not negate its desirability nor that it should sought.

REFERENCES

1. AAA FASC, 'Evaluating Concepts-based *vs.* Rules-based Approaches to Standard Setting', *Accounting Horizons,* March 2003.
2. Alexander, D., 'Legal Certainty, European-ness and Real Politick', *Accounting in Europe,* 2006.
3. Alexander, D., and E.Jermakowicz, 'A True and Fair View of the Principles/Rules Debate', *Abacus,* June 2006.
4. Bagnoli, M., and S.G. Watts, 'Conservative Accounting Choices', *Management Science,* May 2005.
5. Barlev, B., and J.R. Haddad, 'Harmonization, Comparability, and Fair Value Accounting', *Journal of Accounting,* Auditing and Finance, Summer 2007.
6. Barth, M., 'Including Estimates of the Future in Today's Financial Statements', *Accounting Horizons,* September 2006.
7. Barth, M., 'Standard Setting Measurement Issues and the Relevance of Research' *Accounting and Business Research,* Vol. 37, No.3, 2007.
8. Beechy,T., 'Accounting Standards: Rules, Principles, or Wild Guesses?', *Candadian Perspectives on Accounting,* Vol. 4, No.2, 2005.

9. Benston, G.J., M. Broomwich and A. Wagenhofer, 'Principles *VS.* Rules-based Accounting Standards: The FASB's Standard Setting Strategy' *Abacus,* June 2006.

10. Bonham, M. *et al.*, International GAAP 2009, John Wiley & Sons, 2009.

11. Bratton, W. W., 'Enron, Sarbanes-Oxley and Accounting: Rules *VS.* Principles Versus Rent', *Villanova Law Review,* Vol. 48, No.4, 2003.

12. Bromwich, M., 'Fair Values: Imaginary Prices and Mystical Markets—A Clarificatory Review', in P.Walton (ed), *The Routledge Companion to Fair Value and Financial Reporting,* Routledge, 2007.

13. Bullen, H.G., and K. Crook, 'Revisiting the Concepts', FASB/IASB, 2005.

14. Chambers, R.J., 'Accounting Evaluation and Economic Behaviour', Prentice-Hall, 1966.

15. Choi, Y.C., and I.Mc Carthy, 'FASB Proposes Principles-Based Approach to US Standard Setting', *Bank Accounting and Finance,* February 2003.

16. Cunningham, L.A., 'A Prescription to Retire the Rhetoric of Principles-based Systems in Corporate Law, Securities Regulation and Accounting, Boston College Law School, Legal Studies Research Paper Series, *Research Paper* 127, 2007.

17. Dichev, I.D., 'On the Balance Sheet-based Model of Financial Reporting', *Accounting Horizons,* December 2008.

18. DiPiazza, S.A., Jr, *et al.*, Principles-based Accounting Standards, White Paper Delivered by the CEOs of the International Audit Networks at the Global Public Policy Symposium, January 2008.

19. Dopuch, N., and S.Sunder, 'FASB's Statements on Objectives and Elements of Financial Accounting: A Review', *The Accounting Review,* January 1980.

20. Edwards, E.O., and P.W. Bell, 'The Theory and Measurement of Business Income, University of California Press, 1961.

21. Ernst &Young, How Fair is Fair Value?, IFRS Stakeholder Series, Ernst & Young, 2005.

22. Ewert, R., and A.Wagenhofer, 'Economic Effects of Tightening Accounting Standards to Restrict Earnings Management', *The Accounting Review,* October 2005.

23. FASB, 'FASB Discussion Memorandum, Conceptual Framework for Financial Accounting and Reporting : Elements of Financial Statements and Their Measurement, FASB, 1976.

____,Proposal, Principles-based Approach to U.S. Standard Setting, FASB, 1976.

____, FASB Response to SEC Study on the Adoption of a Principles-based Accounting Systems, FASB, 2004.

24. Financial Stability Forum, 'Report of the Financial Stability Forum on Enhancing Market and Institutional Resilience, 2008.

25. Gebhardt, G., and G. Dean, 'Commentary on Siena Open Forum: Conceptual Framework', *Abacus*, June 2008.

26. Guenther, D.A., 'Financial Reporting and Analysis', McGraw-Hill, 2005.

27. Healy, P.M. and K.G. Palepu, 'Effectiveness of Accounting-based Dividend Covenants', *Journal of Accounting and Economics*, January 1990.

28. IASB, 'Conceptual Framework-Qualitative Characteristics 1: Relevance and Reliability (Agenda Paper 7)', Information for Observers, 17 May 2005a.

___, 'Conceptual Framework-Qualitative Characteristics 3: The Relationships Between Qualitative Characteristics (Agenda Paper 7A), Information for Observers, 20 July 2005b.

___,'Conceptual Framework-Qualitative Characteristics 5: The Process for Assessing Qualitative Characteristics (Agenda Paper 8), *Information for Observers*, 19 October 2005c.

___, 'Discussion Paper-Measurement Bases for Financial Accounting-Measurement on Initial Recognition, IASB, 2005d.

___, Exposure Draft of an Improved Conceptual Framework for Financial Reporting, IASB, 2008.

29. ICAS, 'Principles Not Rules: A Question of Judgement, ICAS, 2006a.

___, Principles-based or Rules-based Accounting Standards? A Question of Judgement', ICAS, 2006b.

30. IFRIC, Real Estate Sales (Agenda Paper 3), Information for Observers, September 2006.

31. Johnson, L.T., 'Understanding the Conceptual Framework, Article from The FASB Report', 28 December 2004.

___, 'Relevance and Reliability, Article from The FASB Report', 28 February 2005.

32. Joyce, E.J., R.Libby and S.Sunder, 'Using the FASB's Qualitative Characteristics in Accounting Pollicy Choices', *Journal of Accounting Research*, Autumn 1982.

33. Kivi, L.,P.Smith and C.Wagner, 'Principles-based Standards and the Determination of Control for Consolidation', *CPA Journal,* May 2004.

34. Laux,C., and C.Leuz, 'The Crisis of Fair Value Accounting: Making Sense of the Recent Debate', *Accounting, Organizations and Society,* August-October 2009.

35. Leftwich, R., 'Accounting Information in Private Markets', *The Accounting Review,* January 1983.

36. Lennard, A., 'Stewardship and the Objectives of Financial Statements: A Comment on IASB's Preliminary Views on an Improved Conceptual Framework for Financial Reporting: The Objectives of Financial Reporting and Qualitative Characteristics of Decision-Useful Financial Reporting Information', *Accounting in Europe,* June 2007.

37. Mason, A.K., and M.Gibbins, 'Professional Judgement in Financial Reporting', Canadian Institute of Chartered Accountants, 1988.

___, 'Judgement and U.S. Accounting Standards', Accounting Horizons, June 1991.

38. McBarnet, D., and C.Whelan, 'The Elusive Spirit of the Law: Firmalism and the Struggle for Legal Control', *Modern Law Review,* November 1991.

39. Moonitz, M., 'The Basic Postulates of Accounting', *Accounting Research Study* No.1, AICPA, 1961.

40. Ng.M., 'The Future of Standard Setting', *CPA Journal,* January 2004.

41. Paton, W.A., and A.C. Littleton, 'An Introduction to Corporate Accounting Standards' American Accounting Association Monograph No.3, 12th Printing (1st printing, 1940), *American Accounting Association,* 1965.

42. Penno, M.C., 'Rules and Accounting: Vagueness in Conceptual Frameworks', *Accounting Horizons,* March 2003.

43. Previts, G.J. and B.D.Merino, 'A History of Accountancy in the United States: The Cultural Significance of Accounting', Ohio State University Press, 1998.

44. Psaros, J., 'Do Principles-based Accounting Standards Lead to Biased Financial Reporting? An Australian Experiment', *Accounting and Finance,* September 2007.

45. Raz, J., 'Legal Principles and the Limits of Law', *Yale Law Journal,* April 1972.

46. Rentfro, R., and K.L.Hooks, 'The Effect of Professional Judgement on Financial Reporting Comparability', *Journal of Accounting and Finance Research,* Summer 2004.

47. Ronen, J., 'To Fair Value or Not to Fair Value: A Broader Perspective', *Abacus,* June 2008.

48. Schipper, K., 'Principles-based Accounting Standards', *Accounting Horizons,* March 2003.

49. SEC, 'Study Pursuant to Section 108(d) of the Sarbanes-Oxley Act of 2002 on the Adoption by the United States Financial Reporting System of a Principles-based Accounting System, 2003.

50. Smith, C., and J.Warner, 'On Financial Contracting: An Analysis of Bond Covenants', *Journal of Financial Economics,* June 1979.

51. Solomons, D., 'The FASB's Conceptual Framework: An Evaluation', *Journal of Accountancy*', June 1986.

52. Sprouse, R., and M. Moonitz, 'A Tentative Set of Broad Accounting Principles: An Accounting Research Study, AICPA, 1962.

53. Tsakumis, G.T., T.Doupinik and C.P.Agodia, 'Principles-based *VS.* Rules-based Accounting Standards: The Influence of Standard Precision and Audit Committee Strength on Financial Reporting Decision', AAA 2009.

54. Tweedie, D., 'Oversight Hearing on Accounting and Investor Protection Issues Raised by Enron and Other Public Companies', Prepared Statement of Sir David Tweedie, Chairman of the International Accounting Standards Board, and Former Chairman of the United Kingdom's Accounting Standards Board, 14 February 2002.

___, 'Take it from the Top', A Plus, June 2005.

___, 'Can Global Standards be Principle-based?', *The Journal of Applied Research in Accounting and Finance,* July 2007.

55. Walton, P., 'Fair Value and Executory Contracts: Moving the Boundaries in International Financial Reporting', *Accounting and Business Research,* December 2006.

56. Watts, R., and J.Zimmerman, '*Positive Accounting Theory*', Prentice-Hall, 1986.

57. Whittington, G., 'Fair Value and the IASB/FASB Conceptual Framework Project: An Alternative View', *Abacus,* June 2008.

A Study on Accounting Standards for Intangible Assets

Dr. Fisseha Girmay Tessema,
Dr. Aravind S.,
Dr. P. Paramashivaiah

ABSTRACT

Accounting is often criticized for omitting intangible assets from the balance sheet. Many commentators view the omission of intangible assets from the balance sheet as a glaring deficiency. Accounting is utilitarian so the accounting research question is developing accounting that handles intangible assets that helps to analyze the value of the firm. With growth of global markets the service sector and the level of mergers and acquisitions, intangibles assets have become increasingly important for assessing the total value of a company. It is not only the tangible but also the intangible asset that should be considered.

With growth of global markets the service sector and the level of mergers and acquisitions, intangibles assets have become increasingly important for assessing the total value of a company. It is not only the tangible but also the intangible asset that should be considered.

Keywords: Accounting, Intangible Assets, Global Finance, Growth, Balance Sheet.

Introduction to Intangible Assets

According to Sec 211 of the Companies Act 1956, financial statements must give true and fair view of the state of affairs of the company. All matters which affect the financial position of the business have to be disclosed. The assets & liabilities have to be properly valued so that balance sheet discloses the true and fair financial position of the business.

According to Accounting Principles Board statement No. 4 assets refers to "Economic resources of an enterprises that one recognized and measured deferred charges.

According to the Institute of Chartered Accountants of India, the term assets refers to tangible objects or intangible rights owned by an enterprise and carrying probable future benefits.

Intangible Asset: An asset that can neither be seen nor touched. The most common of these are goodwill & intellectual properties such as patent, trademark and copy rights. Goodwill is probably the most intangible and invisible of all assets and no document provide of the existence and its commercial value.

Most of the companies have avoided to report in a comprehensive way about their intangible assets.

The importance of intangibles is widely acknowledged but identifying, measuring and reporting intangibles have raised questions.

This chapter scans through the accounting practices for intangibles AS 26 & IAS 38. (*see classification assets on next page*)

Objectives

- To Know a brief history of intangible assets valuation
- To Understanding objective of accounting standard of intangible asset and know key terms relevant intangible assets.
- To Review the IAS/IFRS standards that support recognition.

Research Methodology

- The research is a descriptive research, where the description of the state of affairs as it exists at present.

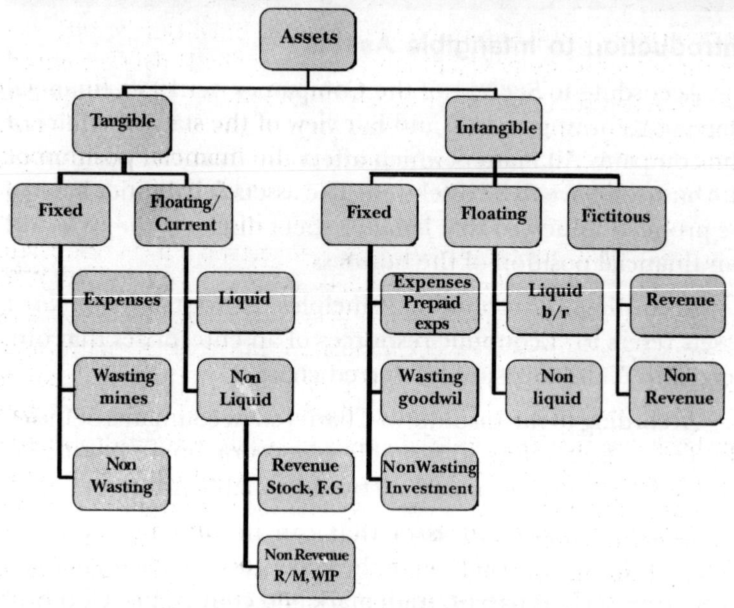

Classification of Assets

- The purpose of research is to report what has happened or what is happening. This may not cover all aspects of the topic for the study.
- Conclusions hereby based on observations and data collected from secondary sources.

Intangible Assets

According to Kohler, an intangible asset is "A capital asset having no physical existence, its value being dependent on the rights that possession confers upon the power.

Intangible assets are defined as identifiable non-monetary assets that can not be such touched or physically measured, which are created through time and or effort & that are identifiable as a separate asset.

Intangible Assets can be Acquired by

- Separate purchases as part of a business combination.

- As part of a business combination.
- By a Government Grant.
- By Exchange of asset.
- Self creation.

Intangible Assets

- Goodwill
- Patents
- Copyright
- Trademark
- Computer software
- Customer list
- Mortgage servicing rights
- Licenses
- Import quotas
- Franchises
- Marketing rights
- Motion picture films

Characteristics of Intangible Assets

- Non-monetary asset.
- It should not have any physical substance.
- It has use in the operating activities.
- Identify control future economic benefits.

Accounting for Intangible Assets

The accounting for intangible assets must be considered in context of the objectives of the financial statements as a whole. One of the objectives is to provide the users the financial statement with useful and reliable information to facilitate their decision making process.

Accounting for intangibles is subjective and complex. Intangible can be identifiable or un-identifiable externally or internally generated.

Accounting treatment of intangibles assets are base on the accounting standards developed of institute of chartered accountants of India.

AS 26- It is quite in line with IAS 38.

Intangible Assets that are Covered by other Accounting Standards

- AS2 — Valuation of Inventories
- AS7 — Accounting for construction contracts
- AS19 — Leases
- AS14 — Accounting for Amalgamators
- AS21 — Consolidated financial statements
- AS22 — Accounting for taxes on income, financial assets, and mineral rights

AS 26

Came in to effect in respect of expenditure incurred on intangibles items during accounting periods commencing on or after 01/04/2003 and is mandatory to Applicability.

Enterprises whole equity or debt securities are listed on a recognized stock exchange.

All other commercial, Industrial and business reporting enterprises whose turnover for the accounting period exceeds 50 crore.

Other enterprises, the accounting standard comes into effect in respect of expenditure incurred on intangible items during accounting periods commencing on 01/04/04.

Recognition and Initial Measurement of an Intangible Asset

1. An intangible assets should be recognized only of the cost of the asset can be measured reliably and future economic benefits that are attributable to the asset will flow into enterprise.
2. An intangible asset should be measured initially at cost.

3. Internally generated goodwill should not be recognized as an asset.

4. An enterprise should assess the probability of future economic benefits using reasonable and supportable assumption.

5. No intangible asset arising from research should be recognized.

6. An intangible asset arising from development phase of an internal project should be recognized if an enterprise can demonstrated on technical feasibility, sale, probable future economic benefit availability of adequate technical, financial, and other resource and ability to measure the expenditure.

Recognition of an Expense

If the requisite conditions are met the subsequent expenditure should be added to the cost of intangible asset.

After initial recognition of an intangible asset, it should be carried at its cost less any accumulation.

Amortization

1. The depreciable amount of an intangible asset should be allocated on a systematic basis over the best estimate of its useful life.

2. Amortization method used should reflect the pattern in which the assets economic benefits are consumed by the enterprise.

3. It control over the future economic benefits from an intangible asset is achieved through legal rights that have been granted for a fixed period, the useful life of the intangible asset should not exceed the period of legal rights.

Residual Value

Of an intangible asset should be assumed to be zero unless there is a commitment by a third party to purchase the asset at the end of its useful life or there is an active market for the asset.

- Review of Amortization period and method
- To be reviewed at least of each financial year end

- Recoverability of the carrying amount — Impairment of losses
- An enterprise should estimate the recoverable amount of the following intangible assets at least each financial year.

Retirement and Disposals

When no future economic benefits are expected from its use and subsequent disposals.

Disclosures

The financial statements should disclose the useful lives or the amortization rates, amortization methods, gross carrying amount, accumulated amortization, reconciliation of the carrying amounts It should also disclose: Amortization of intangible asset over more than 10 years a description, the carrying amount and the amount of commitment for the acquisition.

R&D Expenditure

Aggregate amount of R&D expenditure recognized as an expense.

Transitional Provisions

Intangible Asset Valuation

For valuation purpose intangible asset can be classified into

i. Identifiable intangible asset.

ii. Unidentifiable intangible asset.

Identifiable intangible asset are those which can be identified as distinct and separable property rights.

- Ex patent, trademark, copyright etc.

Unidentifiable intangible assets are those which are not capable of being identified easily. They can not be acquired individually.

Good will: An intangible asset arising from business connection or trade name or reputation of an enterprise. Business is purchased the cost of goodwill is excess of purchase consideration over not tangible asset acquired by the business.

Self generated — At the time of admission retirement or sale of business.

Patent: Grant of right by the government giving owner the exclusive right to manufacture and sell particular invention.

- Purchase — cost is measured by purchase price.
- Developed — Include direct legal and other costs in obtaining patent. No laboratory cost.

Copy Right: Excusive right to publish sell or control literary artistic products for a certain period — cost less any amount amortized.

Preliminary Expenditure: Expenses incurred at the time of promotion or incorporation of a co. written off out of profits over the period.

Conclusion

With growth of global markets the service sector and the level of mergers and acquisitions, intangibles assets have become increasingly important for assessing the total value of a company. It is not only the tangible but also the intangible asset that should be considered.

REFERENCES

1. Alexander, D., 'Legal Certainty, European-ness and Real Politick', *Accounting in Europe*, 2006.
2. Alexander, D., and E. Jermakowicz, 'A True and Fair View of the Principles/Rules Debate', *Abacus*, June 2006.
3. Bagnoli, M., and S.G. Watts, 'Conservative Accounting Choices', *Management Science*, May 2005.
4. Cunningham, L.A., 'A Prescription to Retire the Rhetoric of Principles-based Systems in Corporate Law, Securities Regulation and Accounting, Boston College Law School, *Legal Studies Research Paper Series*, Research Paper 127, 2007.
5. Dichev, I.D., 'On the Balance Sheet-based Model of Financial Reporting', *Accounting Horizons*, December 2008.
6. Ernst & Young, How Fair is Fair Value?, *IFRS Stakeholder Series*, Ernst & Young, 2005.

7. Ewert, R., and A. Wagenhofer, 'Economic Effects of Tightening Accounting Standards to Restrict Earnings Management', *The Accounting Review,* October 2005.
8. Financial Stability Forum, 'Report of the Financial Stability Forum on Enhancing Market and Institutional Resilience, 2008.
9. Gebhardt, G., and G. Dean, 'Commentary on Siena Open Forum: Conceptual Framework', *Abacus,* June 2008.
10. Whittington, G., 'Fair Value and the IASB/FASB Conceptual Framework Project: An Alternative View', *Abacus,* June 2008.

International Financial Reporting Standards

Implementation Challenges and Implications on Key Sectors in India

Prof. Trilok Nath Shukla,
Miss. Archita De

ABSTRACT

Indian companies has surpassed in several sectors of the industry and to stay as a leader in the international market. India opted the changes it need to interface Indian stakeholders', the international stakeholders' and comply with the financial reporting in a language that is understandable to all of them. In response to the need several Indian companies have already been providing their financial statements as per US GAAP and/or IFRS on voluntary basis. But, however this is becoming more of a necessity then just being a best practice.

In the coming years, critical decisions will need to be made regarding the use of global accounting standards in India. Market participants will be called upon to determine whether achieving a uniform set of high-quality global accounting standards is feasible, what sort of investments would be required to achieve that outcome, and whether it is a desirable goal in the first place. This dialogue will be critical to the future of financial reporting and of fundamental importance to the long-term strength and stability of the global capital markets.

Performance measures, based on Indian GAAP may need revisiting as it may change in IFRS adoption by fair amount on account of valuation aspect. Expectation of investor and market will also be required to be of paramount importance to manage in the adoption of process.

The effect of adopting IFRS will depend on each individual organization's circumstances and business practices. That being said, changing to IFRS may affect certain industries more than others. Some of the key sectors on which the implication of IFRS and the challenges faced by them are discussed in this article are:

Banking	Information Technology	Technology
Pharmaceutical	Real estate	Retail
Telecome, Tech and Media	Extractive	Microfinance
Public Sector Units		

Introduction

The growing acceptance of International Financial Reporting Standards (IFRS) as a basis for U.S. financial reporting represents a fundamental change for the U.S. accounting profession. Today nearly 100 countries require or allow the use of IFRS for the preparation of financial statements by publicly held companies. In the United States, the Securities and Exchange Commission (SEC) is consid standard-setting process began several decades ago as an effort by industrialized nations to create standards that could be used by developing and smaller nations unable to establish their own accounting standards. But as the business world became more global, regulators, investors, large companies and auditing firms began to realize the importance of having common standards in all areas of the financial reporting chain.

Global Foot Prints of IFRS

In last few years, because of emergence of the Global Economy and growing integration of world's capital markets, financial reporting have undergone significant changes. Many market participants are considering the question of whether it is possible or desirable to move toward a single "globally accepted financial reporting standard" so that these entities' can speak a uniform global 'language' for financial reporting.

The proponents of this idea argue that a uniform set of global accounting standards, supported by strong corporate governance, independent standard-setting and a sound regulatory framework, could benefit investors and businesses alike. Others suggest that trying to establish a uniform set of global standards would run the risk of overlooking the unique economic, political, cultural, legal and regulatory realities that exist in different nations and regions across the globe.

Over the years the use of IFRS has emerged as widely used and accepted standard in the world with more than 12,000 companies and over 100 countries accepting and mandating its implementation. India aims to be joining IFRS club starting FY 2011.

Development in India

The Indian GAAP is influenced by several standard setters and influenced by Statute, namely Companies Act, Income Tax Act, Banking Regulation Act, Insurance Act etc and directions from regulatory bodies like RBI, SEBI, IRDA. The legal or regulatory requirement will prevail over the IFRS requirement, in case of conflicts. Therefore, preconditions for IFRS adoption by India to be effective need amendments in required legislation and clarity on impact of IFRS adoption on Direct and Indirect taxes, especially transactions recorded at fair values.

Institute of Chartered Accountants of India is actively promoting the IASB's pronouncements in the country with a view to facilitating global harmonization of Accounting Standards and ICAI has pronounced that Indian GAAP will converge into IFRS with effect from April 1, 2011. With the decibel level increasing on the IFRS (International Financial Reporting Standards) front, a natural anxiety among investors is about how the adoption of global norms will impact the different sectors.

IFRS Impact on the Banking Sector

In addition to the several challenges along the path to convergence that are applicable to all companies, banking companies in India face certain additional challenges. These include:

- In addition to the general accounting standards and practices that constitute Indian GAAP, banking companies are currently required to adhere to accounting policies and principles that are prescribed by the Reserve Bank of India (RBI).
- Application of IFRS in areas such as provision for loan losses and impairment of investments generally requires a high level of judgment and would require significant changes in the financial reporting processes (for example, to estimate cash flows that will be recovered including through sale of collateral).
- Assuming that India converges with IFRS using the transition provision of IFRS. First-time Adoption of International Financial Reporting Standards, several provisions of IFRS would need to be retroactively applied, subject to available exemptions under IFRS.
- International Accounting Standards 39 (IAS 39) on Financial Instruments: Substantially all the assets and liabilities of banking companies comprise financial instruments that would be governed the provisions of IAS 39.
- Similarly, IAS 39 requires extensive use of fair valuation. Given the economic environment in India and lack of relatively developed financial markets for certain foreign exchange and interest rate instruments applications of these required fair valuation techniques possess additional implementation challenges.
- By virtue of operating in a regulated industry banking companies are subject to regulatory reviews and inspection and are also subject to minimum capital requirements.. The regulatory review process would need to be adjusted to acknowledge the inherent judgments involved in the application of IFRS. Additionally, application of IFRS may result in higher loan losses and impairment charges thereby impacting available capital and capital adequacy ratio. Similarly, use of fair values would introduce additional volatility in reported capital with its consequent impact on capital adequacy.

Technical Accounting Challenges for Banks

1. *Loan/Investment Impairment*

Should there be an expectation that all contractual cash flows would not be recovered (or recovered without full future interest applications) an account would be classified as impaired and impairment be measured on present value basis using the effective interest rate of the exposure as the discount rate. The aim of an individual or collective assessment is to capture the incurred loss for a specified portfolio. No provisions are permitted for future or expected losses. For investment a similar analysis is conducted the key difference being that the fair value of the investment is also considered as an input in addition to the financial /credit standing of the issuer. The bedrock of this impairment assessment is a system that considers all the facts and circumstances and requires the use of informed judgement. This aspect represents the most significant difference from Indian GAAP for banks in India. Current Indian GAAP/RBI guidelines require a limited use of judgement are mechanistic in nature with prescribed provisioning rates.

2. *Required Use of Fair Value for More Financial Instruments*

Under IFRS there may be a significant increase in the extent that fair value measurement needs to be used. For instance all financial assets and liabilities will need to be initially measured at fair value. While in a number of instances fair values may be represented by transaction prices, the onus on banks will be to prove that transactions prices represent fair value. In addition, there will be a number of instances where unrealized gains can/should be recognized: for example, trading instruments and those where the bank elects the fair value option. Further due to the stringent criteria a prescribed under IFRS, a Held to Maturity (HTM) classification, is unlikely to be available leading to fair value measurement for a substantial part of the portfolio. Again this is a significant shift from current accounting treatment under Indian GAAP.

3. *Derivatives and Hedge Accounting*

Under IFRS all derivatives are recognized on the balance sheet at fair values with changes in fair value being recognized generally in the income statement other than in the case of a qualifying cash flow hedge relationship. Application of hedge accounting does reduce the income statement volatility induced by the fair value measurement of derivatives but comes with significant strings attached in the form of documentation hedge effectiveness testing and ineffectiveness measurement. In addition embedded derivative require to be separated from their host contracts and be accounted for separately. In contrasts, current Indian GAAP does not specifically address the more difficult to apply provisions of fair value and hedge accounting.

4. *De-recognition of Financial Assets*

Under IFRS de recognition of financial assets is complex multi — layered area with the de-recognition decision dependent largely on whether there has been a transfer of risks and rewards. If the assessment of the transfer of risks and rewards is not conclusive an assessment of control and the extent of continuing involvement is required to be performed. In many cases this cannot be restricted to qualitative assessment and need to be necessarily a quantities assessment. A major area impacted would be securitization activity most Indian securitization vehicles are currently structured to meet Indian GAAP de-recognition norms. Substantially all those securitization vehicles would collapse into the transferor's balance sheet and assets would fail the de-recognition test under IFRS.

5. *Consolidation of Entities*

Under IFRS consolidation is not driven purely by the ownership structure of an entity. Instead the focus is more on the power to control an entity to obtain economic benefits this power to control could be expressed as ownership of equity securities but is not limited to it. For instance this will include a consideration of currently exercisable potential voting rights/ shares; management and other agreements de facto control and other arrangement that provide the power to control an entity. IFRS also provides guidance on how consolidation decisions for special purpose entities should be arrived at.

Impact of IFRS on IT Sector

The transition to International Financial Reporting Standards (IFRS) is all set to impact the revenue top-line being reported by IT companies. India Inc is all set to converge with International Financial Reporting Standards (IFRS), effective April 1, 2011, and since comparatives are required, the opening IFRS bell will ring on April 1, 2010. IFRS is a very different accounting framework since it focuses more on substance and is largely fair value driven, which is a significant departure from the current accounting milieu.

First and foremost, IFRS may have a significant impact on the revenue top-line being reported by technology companies. Technology companies enter into lump sum contracts for sale of licenses, implementation fees, warranty, maintenance and free upgrade services, etc., over a period of time.

Under IFRS, a key issue will be to determine whether the components of a single transaction can be separated from an obligations performance standpoint *i.e.* from a technical and commercial perspective. In such instances, bundled contracts and multiple offerings under a package will require fair valuation of different components and revenues would be recognized accordingly. Indian GAAP does not provide any specific guidance on this and, therefore, inconsistent practices are presently being followed by various companies. Some companies defer the revenue recognition till the entire project is completed. Other companies recognize revenues and provide for costs associated with pending post-sale contractual obligations. Very recently, the research committee of the ICAI has come out with a technical guide on revenue recognition for software companies, which is very similar to SOP 97-2 followed in US GAAP. However, this is not a notified accounting literature under Indian GAAP and companies may not be required to follow it mandatorily.

The other area where IT companies will get impacted is stock options. Under IFRS 2, share-based payments cover non-employees also. If certain non-employee obligations are settled through ESOP, IFRS will require fair value accounting for such options and cost differential between grant price and fair value will have to be recognized. Moreover, subsidiaries will need to account for the ESOP costs for options granted to its employees by the parent company, with corresponding impact in capital contribution by the parent as per requirement of IFRIC 11. This is likely to have a major impact in the case of many IT multinational subsidiaries operating in India, since many of their senior executives are given stock options in the parent company listed in the US/global markets, and where such accounting was not required under Indian GAAP so far.

Another key aspect is that Indian GAAP allows intrinsic method of accounting, in which case the ESOP cost is generally lower since it only takes into account the value of option as at the date of its grant and does not capture the likely accretion in fair value over the entire vesting period. Share based payment costs are expected to increase on application of the IFRS, which will eat into the profitability of IT companies.

Large outsourcing contracts are quite common in the IT sector. Often a significant part of the capacity is being utilized by a specific customer or facilities may be specifically earmarked to cater to the needs of a particular client. Usually in such cases, the pricing of the contract is also agreed on special terms, keeping in mind the costs incurred by the IT company in providing such services. In such scenarios, one will have to evaluate whether provision/receipt of services constitutes or contains a lease arrangement under IFRIC 4. Financial statements would change quite significantly if it is determined that such transactions contain an element of lease, particularly if they satisfy the criteria for a finance lease. Under Indian GAAP, such arrangements are normally considered as those for providing services and not a leasing activity.

IFRS entails discounting of future receivables and payables to their current values using expected interest rates. The application of 'time value of money' concept will have impact on the amounts recorded for long-term security deposits, payables falling due after one year and revenues earned in advance for long-term contracts/ arrangements. Imputed interest amounts will also have an impact on profits reported by IT companies.

Last but not the least, large companies with active treasury operations will also have to comply with IAS 39 on financial instruments, particularly with regard to accounting for derivatives. Under IFRS, hedge accounting is permitted for such transactions provided entities have robust documentation and certain conditions are met. Thus, entities will have to put in necessary process in place to satisfy requirements of IAS 39. Most IT companies have huge exposure to currency movements, so they will need to make immediate preparations for the advent of IFRS and start putting in place systems and processes for derivatives (including embedded ones), as well as hedge accounting.

Hence convergence to IFRS is not a mere accounting exercise and will have significant business implications. Hence, companies would augur well to start preparing early and not wait for the last moment to rush to converge.

Impact of IFRS on Technology Companies

Companies with global operations usually grapple with numerous statutory reporting requirements under different accounting standards in each country. In such cases, there are significant benefits that can be gained from transitioning the financial reporting of all global subsidiaries and affiliates to IFRS —including potential for reduced lead time in preparing consolidated financial statements, fewer reconciliation issues, improved controls, reduced personnel costs, and a centralized approach to addressing statutory reporting issues.

With the rapid adoption of IFRS worldwide, the prospect of a 'global GAAP' has moved from a lofty vision to a practical reality. More than 100 countries now require the use of IFRS and it is expected to impact the global capital markets, U.S. public companies, and statutory reporting in the following ways:

IFRS can provide an opportunity to lower the cost of capital by expanding the base for global funding without having to incur additional financial reporting costs. A single global set of accounting standards can encourage both companies and investors to more easily access multiple or foreign markets, in effect, helping to stimulate investment and enabling cross-border capital flows. With the SEC's recent proposal to allow certain U.S. issuers the option of filing IFRS financial statements for years ending on or after December 15, 2009 and other filers likely to follow from 2014 through 2016, IFRS is quickly becoming a reality for U.S. companies. GAAP would be the primary financial reporting languages within their organizations are now faced with learning a new reporting language and dealing with its broad implications. A conversion to IFRS may start with accounting differences and policy choices, but can eventually impact the entire organization. Understanding the impact of IFRS on various aspects of the company such as tax, treasury, and processes and systems is important to preparing for a successful implementation.

Differences Between IFRS and U.S.GAAP

The following are a few key differences that will likely affect many technology companies:

(a) *Revenue Recognition:* IFRS guidance with respect to revenue recognition is much less detailed than U.S.GAAP. IFRS is much more principle-based as compared to U.S. GAAP which provides detailed guidance and rules around the accounting for these types of arrangements. Therefore, in adopting IFRS, companies will have to re-evaluate their existing revenue recognition policies to determine whether they are consistent with the underlying principles in IFRS. Also, changes in revenue recognition will need to be analyzed to determine the effect on the tax method for recognizing income or the cumulative temporary differences resulting from the new book method of accounting in impacted jurisdictions. The implications of this difference extend beyond the accounting of specific transactions and could potentially influence the structure of future contracts.

(b) *Share-based payments:* Similar to U.S. GAAP, IFRS takes a fair value approach to share based payments. However, key differences between IFRS and U.S.GAAP include the attribution method and the calculation of income tax expense related to stock options. Under U.S. GAAP, companies have a choice to use straight-line or accelerated amortization while IFRS requires accelerated amortization only. The tax accounting for options, as currently written under International Accounting Standard (IAS) 12, may lead to more volatility, higher tax expense, and could require significant changes in your software systems in order to track the deferred tax asset. The tax benefit (in the form of a deferred tax asset) for options and other share-based awards under U.S. GAAP is driven off the book expense for the awards, while under IFRS the tax benefit at each reporting date is based on the expected tax deduction, not to exceed the book expense. This may lead to greater volatility in tax expense and may require revamped software capabilities.

(c) *Research and Development Costs:* U.S GAAP requires all costs related to research and development activities to be expensed as incurred, with few exceptions. IFRS differentiates between 'research' and 'development' costs, with development costs capitalized when the technical and economic feasibility of a project can be demonstrated and further prescribed conditions are satisfied.

(d) *Income Taxes:* Under U.S. GAAP, uncertain tax positions have a specifically prescribed methodology to record and disclose companies' tax positions based on a two-step approach for the recognition and measurement of unrecognized tax benefits. Under IFRS, accounting for tax uncertainties reflects management's expectations. Also, IFRS includes a provision defining the tax base in terms of management's 'expected manner of recovery,' whereas U.S. GAAP doesn't specifically define the tax base. Additionally, as many technology companies have significant intercompany transactions, such as those resulting from cost sharing arrangements, it is important to note that U.S. GAAP provides for the deferral of taxes paid on intercompany profits for assets that remain in the group, while IFRS has no such exception.

(e) *Inventory:* IFRS requires that when the circumstances that previously caused inventories to be written down below cost no longer exist, or when there is clear evidence of an increase in net realizable value because of changed economic circumstances, the amount of the write-down is reversed (*i.e.*, the reversal is limited to the amount of the original write-down) so that the new carrying amount is the lower of the historical cost and the revised net realizable value.

(*f*) *Asset Impairments:* The carrying value of the asset is compared with the undiscounted value of the future cash flows and if the carrying value is higher, the asset is written down to fair value. Under IFRS, the carrying value is compared with the asset's recoverable amount (defined as the higher of the asset's fair value and its value in use— which is based on discounted future cash flows). If the carrying value is higher, the asset is written down to the recoverable amount. The ultimate effect is that impairment is likely to occur sooner under IFRS, but the amount of impairment in a given accounting period may be lower. In addition, IFRS requires that under certain conditions, a previously-recognized impairment (other than those relating to goodwill) may be reversed up to the original value of the asset. Thus, under IFRS, any asset impairments will need to be tracked to determine the appropriate amount of any future reversal. Under U.S.GAAP, reversals of previous impairments to long-lived assets are not permitted.

(g) *Human Resources:* IFRS will likely influence your hiring, training and compensation practices. In many cases, reporting under IFRS will change the bottom line that serves as the basis of many compensation plans. Having a finance team that understands how IFRS will impact the financial statements will allow a smooth transition to revised compensation plans that sales people and executives will be able to understand.

(h) *Legal:* An IFRS conversion will potentially impact a number of business arrangements. Accordingly, involvement of the legal team is a key consideration. The legal counsel is already aware that the technology industry has a propensity for joint ventures, profit-sharing, and other collaborative arrangements. The contractual underpinnings of all these relationships will need to be revisited. It's not hard to imagine that if a conversion to IFRS has an impact on the bottom line numbers, then the results of the partnering arrangements will change. The legal team should take a proactive approach to heading off problems resulting from changes in outcomes and steering clear of potential litigation.

(i) *Treasury:* IFRS can also have significant impacts on your treasury function. Many global lenders, global private equity firms, and international exchanges require or prefer IFRS reporting due to its increased transparency into fair values and comparability to other investments or companies. Thus, these sources potentially become new avenues for capital funding, particularly in the current U.S. dollar environment.

(j) *Tax:* Understanding tax consequences of IFRS will be critical for finance and tax executives to help manage and plan tax strategies for the organization. As with any tax accounting issue, the effort for an IFRS conversion will require close collaboration between the finance and tax departments. Significant differences between U.S. GAAP and IFRS that may require considerable tax analysis will include revenue recognition principles; revaluation of property, plant, and equipment; component depreciation; inventory valuation; sale and leaseback transactions; pension liabilities and assets; business combinations; research and development costs; and share-based compensation. It is incumbent upon the tax director to evaluate the potential impact and determine whether there may be opportunities to mitigate any detrimental results by accelerating tax planning strategies to occur prior to conversion to IFRS.

(k) *Information Technology:* Changes in accounting policies and financial reporting processes can also have a significant imact on a company's financial systems and reporting infrastructure. These changes may require some adjustments to finacial reporting systems, existing interfaces, and underlying databases to incorporate specific data to support IFRS reporting. Executives will need to collaborate with their IT

counterparts to review systems implications of IFRS. Current systems may not have the functionality to handle IFRS requirements, so changes in financial information requirements due to IFRS should be identified and the impact of these requirements on the existing data models should be assessed. Valuation systems and actuarial models will also need to be evaluated to accommodate IFRS changes.

IFRS Impact on the Pharmaceutical Industry

Companies that think they might be eligible to adopt IFRS would be required to make a written submission to the staff on their eligibility and receive a no-objection letter from the staff. More than 100 countries already require or permit IFRS or a national variant for reporting by listed companies, while others, including China, India, Japan, and Canada, have plans to adopt IFRS or converge with IFRS by 2011. The conversion of U.S.-based pharmaceutical companies to a single set of global accounting standards should make it easier for them to compare financial results with those of their foreign counterparts and facilitate access to foreign capital markets—and eventually reduce compliance costs.

Revenue recognition for collaborations and strategic alliances, which often provide a critical source of new compounds and drugs for companies, could differ considerably under IFRS, as revenue from certain elements of these arrangements may be recognized differently under IFRS than under U.S. GAAP Collaboration and alliance agreements will have to be reviewed for changes in accounting, particularly if there are payment metrics based on U.S. GAAP amounts. The key is that IFRS contains only a 'general' principle that multiple-element arrangements should be separated into different units of account; interpretative or industry-specific guidance is limited. This is less restrictive than the criteria for separation under U.S. GAAP. Under IFRS, acquired intangibles are capitalized when specified criteria are met, even if the development of the drug or compound is not completed. Once a company converts to IFRS, it is required to use the same cost method for all inventories of a similar nature. Any inventory write-downs must be reversed later on if the value of the inventory recovers.

For management, a thorough understanding of IFRS is critical when negotiating future arrangements, particularly licensing deals and collaborations, since certain technology development costs currently expensed under U.S. GAAP may need to be capitalized and amortized under IFRS. Management will also need to communicate how its U.S. GAAP results will translate into IFRS results—companies cannot risk having markets misinterpret results. In addition to accounting changes, companies will have to review and assess contractual arrangements to account for changes under IFRS. They will need to update existing debt covenants that are based on U.S. GAAP information and compensation and benefit plans that are based on U.S. GAAP performance measures to account for IFRS-based metrics. Another large-scale process change involves the modification of IT systems to accommodate IFRS. Going forward, the effect of IFRS must be taken into consideration when making an IT system change. Management will need to consider new data requirements under IFRS and changes to accounts and account mapping, as well as internal and external reporting packages and budget and forecasting packages.

Development agreements may be structured such that the party performing the development incurs short term losses on a development project but has access to future revenues when a product is eventually produced and marketed. The biotech company bears greater risk in developing the product but may receive a greater share of future benefits at a later stage. Fees to be received after the development period will often not be in return for a service. When considering the expected benefits under the contract (IAS 37.68) the amounts expected over the entire contract should be taken into account and not only those amounts receivable over the development period.

Generally a company would not have an onerous contract if it had a significant exposure to the risks and rewards of ownership of the asset under development. These rewards may take many different forms including royalties and/or manufacturing fees at greater than commercial rates. The probability of future rewards may be slim, however that is part and parcel of the business of pharmaceutical research and is the risk taken by all companies in performing research and development work. This risk is generally factored into price negotiations such that at the outset of a contract the expected benefits, on a weighted average probability basis, exceed the potential costs of fulfilling the contract [IAS 37.10].

The process of IFRS transition will require careful consideration. Pharmaceuticals companies will most likely need to provide three years of comparative financial statements (as they currently do) in the period of first-time adoption.

IFRS Impact on the Real Estate Industry

Some of India's large real estate firms are seeking exemption from adopting the proposed International Financial Reporting Standards (IFRS) from the next fiscal year. All real estate companies that form part of the NSE's Nifty-50 or BSE's Sensex-30, will have to report financial returns according to the stringent revenue recognition norms laid down by the IFRS. For years, developers in India have been recognizing revenue the moment an agreement for sale of a flat is signed. They do this after completing about 20-25 per cent of the total construction work, mainly to assure investors that the project is safe. So, under India's GAAP, revenue is earned the moment an under-construction flat is booked. However, under the IFRS, only when an apartment is constructed and ownership rights are transferred will revenue from such transaction be recognized. According to industry experts, the consequences will also extend to structuring of ESOPs schemes, training of employees, modification of IT systems and tax planning. Companies will also need to communicate the impact of IFRS convergence to their investors to ensure they understand the shift from Indian GAAP to IFRS.

Some of the challenges which the builders are facing are having fully-trained finance staff, revenue recognition, as well as knowledge of impact of IFRS on business. In the first phase of the roll-out, the IFRS norms will impact companies with networth of over Rs 1,000 crore or those who have issued Foreign Currency Convertible Bonds (FCCBs) or Global Depository Receipts (GDRs). Having studied the detailed impact of IFRS on the realty sector, Confederation of Real Estate Developers of India (CREDAI) plans to take up the matter with the government.. However, the Institute of Chartered Accountants of India (ICAI) is in no mood to exempt any sector/industry from adopting these standards as it could trigger off an avalanche of such requests from sectors like banking. The more challenging issues in financial reporting and disclosure for real estate companies, which include:

- **Recognition, Measurement and Classifications**

  Measuring investment properties at fair value at each reporting period-end, with fair values either reported *(i)* directly on the balance sheet (and corresponding changes in fair values recorded through the statement of earnings) or *(ii)* in the notes to the financial statements. Ensuring all categories of real estate assets are defined and described properly in the accounting policies.

- **Statement of Earnings**

  Presenting the various components that are part of revenue. The notes and accounting policies should clearly state what is included in revenue on a gross basis, the financial statements need to be clear that the entity acts as a principal rather than as an agent.

- **Acquisitions**

  Considering the implications of the distinct accounting treatment of asset deals or business combinations.

- **Development Property**

  The criteria for real estate transfers in and out of investment property need to be disclosed in the accounting policies.

- **Deferred Tax**

  Disclosing relevant information relating to deferred tax balances: how this balance has been calculated, what the impact is of adjustments on the balance, the impact of different tax rates of efficient structures.

- **Lease incentives**

  Ensuring the accounting for lease incentives is appropriate and the impact on the valuation of real estate assets is appropriately considered and disclosed. A more clear perception on the new standards and its interpretations are given in the tabular form.

Table 10.1: Operating Segments

New Standards and Interpretations

Name	Effective Date (annual period-beginning)	Date of Endorsement by the EU	Application
IFRS8 Operating Segments	1 January 2009	21 November 2007	Mandatory for year ending December 31, 2009 Retrospective
	Summary • Specifies how an entity should report information about its operating segments in annual financial statements and requires an entity to reports selected information about its operating segments in interim financial reports. • Generally, financial information is required to be reported on the same basis as is used internally for evaluating operatng segment performation and deciding how to allocate resources to operting segments. • However, IFRS 8 Does not require an entity to report in information that is not prepared for internal use if the necessary infromation is not avilable and the coast to develop it would be excessive • This standard is only applicable for companies whose equity inqstruments are traded in a public market or entities who are filing financial statements with regulators for purpose of issusing any call of instruments in a public market. **Main Changes** • The Standard replaced IAS 14 and Main Chages relate to: — Identification of segments — Measurement of segment information — Disclosures		

Source:http: //www.deloitte.com/view/en_LU/lu/industries/real-state/article/31c6d4de4e 76210VgnVCM100000ba42f00aRCRD.htm

Table 10.2 Agreements for the Construction of Real Estate

New Standards and Interpretations

Name	Effective Date (annual period-beginning	Date of Endorsement by the EU	Application
IFRIC Interpretation 15 Agreements for the Construction of Real Estate	1 Janunary 2009	22 July 2009	Optional for year ending December 31, 2009 Mandatory for year ending December 31, 2010 Retrospective
	• Specifies whether an agreement for construction of Real Estate is within the scope of IAS 11-Construction contracts or IAS 18-Revenue		

Source: http://www.deloitte.com/view/en_LU/lu/industries/real-estate/article/931c6d4de4e76210VgnVCM100000ba42f00aRCRD.htm

Table 10. 3: Presentation of Financial Statements

Amendments to Existing Standards and Interpretations

Name	Effective Date (annual period-beginning)	Date of Endorsement by the EU	Application
IAS 1 (revised) Presentation of Financial Statements	1 January 2009	17 December 2008	Madalory for year ending December 31, 2009 Restrospective
	• States fundamental principles established for the preparation of the financail statments. including going con-		

Contd..

	cern assumption. consistency in presentation and classification, accrual basis of accounting and materiality • A complete set of financial statement comprises: - A statement of financial position - A statement of comprehensive income - A statement of changes in equity - A statement of cash flows - Noes and - A statement of financial position as at begining of the earliest comparative period*
	Main changes: • New littles (not mandatory): - Balance sheet ⇨ statment of financial position - Cash flow statement ⇨ statement of cash flow • All changes in euity arising from transactions with owners (*i. e.* owner changes in equity) need to be presented separately form non-owners changes in equity • Statement of financial position should include an additional period presented when an entity applies an accounting policy retrospectively or makes a retrospective restatement of items or when it reclassifies items in its financial statements

Source: http://www.deloitte.com/view/en_LU/lu/industries/real-estate/article/ 931c6d4de4e76210VgnVCM100000ba42f00aRCRD.htm

Table 10.4: Capitalization of Borrowing Costs

Amendments to Existing Standards and Interpretations

Name	Effective Date (annual period-beginning	Date of Endorsement by the EU	Application
IAS 23 (revised) Capitalization of Bowrrowing Costs	1 January 2009	10 December 2008	Mandatory for year ending December 31, 2009 Prospective, specific transitional requirements

Contd..

	Main change: Removal of option to expense all borrowing coast. **Summary of the Standard:** • Borrowing costs directly attributable to the acquisition. construction or production of a qualifiying asset are as part of the cost of that assets, but capitalized only when it is probable that these coasts will result in future benefits to the entity and the costs can measured realiably. All other borrowing costs that do not satisfy the conditions for capitalization are expenses when incurred • A qualifying asset is one that necessarily takes a substantial period of time to get it ready for its intened use or sale. Example of qualifying asset includes investment properties

Source: http://www.deloitte.com/view/en_LU/lu/industries/real-estate/article/931c6d4de4e76210VgnVCM100000ba42f00aRCRD.htm

Table 10. 5: Puttable Instruments

Amendments to Existing Standards and Interpretations

Name	Effective Date (annual period-beginning	Date of Endorsement by the EU	Application
IAS 32 (amendment) Puttable Instruments	1 January 2009	21 Janunary 2009	Mandatory for year ending December 31, 2009 Retrospective, specific transitional requirements
	Main change: puttable instruments and instruments that impose on the entity anobligation to deliver a pro-rata share of net assets only on liquidation that: *(a)* Are Subordinate to all other classes of instrument (IAS 32.16A & C *(b)* Meet additional critieria (IAS 32. 16 B & D) Are classified as equity instruments even through they would otherwise meet the definition of a liabiltiy		

Contd..

	• All following five criteria must be met to classify a putable instrument as equity (IAS 32. 16A/B - Entitlement to pro-rate share of met assets on liquidation - In the most subordinate class of instrument, all having identical features - Contains on other obligation that represents a financial liablity - Exprected cash flows are substantially based on profit or loss, recognized net assets or recognizes and unrecognizes net - No other instrument outstanding which cash flows are based assets on the same measures as set out above and has an effect of restrcting fixing return on the puttable instrument **Summary of the standard** • Prescribe principles for classifying and presenting financial instruments as liabilities or equity, and for offsetting financial assets and liabilities

Source: http://www.deloitte.com/view/en_LU/lu/industries/real-estate/article/ 931c6d4de4e76210VgnVCM100000ba42f00aRCRD.htm

IFRS Impact on the Retail Sector

There is a significant difference between the Indian GAAP and IFRS which pose both accounting and business challenges to entities in the real sector. Straight-lining of lease rentals in an operating lease, is required both by Indian GAAP and IFRS. However, under Indian GAAP, not all companies are straight-lining because land is scoped out of AS-19. It may be noted under IFRS there is no exemption.

U.S. GAAP Compared with IFRS

(a) Inventories (IAS 2)

Inventories for retailers are a significant asset, and inventory management is a critical success factor of high performing companies.

Table 10.6: Business Combinations and Consolidation and Separate Financial Statements

Amendments to Existing Standars and Interpretations

Name	Effective Date (annual period-beginning)	Date of Endorsement by the EU	Application
IFRS 3 and IAS 27 (amendment) Business Combinations and Consolidated and Separate Financial Statement	1 July 2009*	3 June 2009	Optional for year ending December 31, 2009 Mandatory for year ending December 31. 2010 Prospective, specific transitional requirements
liability	**Main change:** • Acquisition costs ⇨ Expensed in profit and loss • Contingent consideration⇨Adjustment to recognised in profit or loss • Partial acquisition ⇨ Choice of measurement basis for non-controlling interests • Step acquisition ⇨ Previous/residual holding remeasured to fair value • Transaction with non-controlling interest ⇨ Recognised in equity on goodwill or profit/loss		

* So if the financial year-end is December 31, 2009, then first application is 2010

Source: http://www.deloitte.com/view/en_LU/lu/industries/real-estate/article/ 931c6d4de4e76210VgnVCM100000ba42f00aRCRD.htm

Table 10. 7: Improvement to IFRS 2008 Sales of Assets Held for Rental
Amendments to Existing Standards and Interpretations

Name	Effective Date (annual period beginning)	Date of Endorsement by the EU	Application
IAS 16/IAS 7 (amendment) following Improvements to IFRS 2008 Sales of assets held for rental	1 January 2009	January 23. 2009	Mandatory for year ending December 31. 2009
	Main change: • Entities that routinely sell items of property, plant and equipment that they have previously held for rental, to others, should transfer such assets to inventories at their carrying amount when they ceases to be rented and are held for sale. The proceeds from the sale of such assets should be recognised as reventure in accordance with IAS 18 • Cash payment to manufacture or acquire such assets and cash recepit form rental and sale of such assets are to be included within operating activities		
IAS 40/IAS 16 (amendment) following improvements to IFRS 2008 Property under construction or development for future use as investment property	1 January 2009	January 23. 2009	Mandatory for year ending December 31. 2009 Prospective, specific transititonal requirements
	Main change: • Amendment to bring property under construction or development for development for future use as an investment property within the scope of IAS 40. Such property previously fell within the scope of IAS 16		

Source: http://www.deloitte.com/view/en_LU/lu/industries/real-estate/article/ 931c6d4de4e76210VgnVCM100000ba42f00aRCRD.htm

Table 10. 8: Perspective of Implementing IFRS

Topic
Lease accounting (Discussion paper): • On March 19, 2009, the IASB and the issued a discussion paper outliminary views on accounting model, in connection with lease accounting. The Scope is, however, limited to leassee accounting • The proposed model would eliminate the operating lease classification for lessess. If this proposal were adopted in a final standard. operating leases would no longer be 'off-balance sheet' and rental expenses would on longer be straight lined over the lease tem. Rather, an asset (that will probably be called 'Right to use') and a liability would eb recognised in the statement of financial position of financial position and amortization and interest expense would be recognised in profit and loss
Exposure draft proposing improvements on eleven IFRSs: • On 26 August 2009, the IASB published for comment an exposure draft propsing improvement to eleven IRFSs. • One of the most significant prosposal address the removal of the requirment in IAS 40 Investment property to transfer investment property carried at fair value to investment when it will be developed for sale
Joint arragment (Expected in Q1 2010) • Before: Legal from of agreements ð After. Substance over form: contractual right and obligations agreed by the parties • Before: Choice of equity method or proportionals consolidationð After: Removal of proportionaate consolidation
Exposure draft on Consolidated financial statement(ED 10): • The ED 10 propose a new definition of control (Power to direct the activities of other entities to generate return for the reporting entity) and provided a guidance when a structured entity. an entity had less than a majority of the voting rights, and accessing control of It incldes enhanced disclosures relating to information about 'off balance sheet' activities and effect of on controlling interests and the reporting • It also concluded that reputational risk is not an apropriate basis for consolidation entity should disclose the support provided to unconsolidated structured entities.

Source: http://www.deloitte.com/view/en_LU/lu/industries/real-estate/article/931c6d4de4e76210VgnVCM100000ba42f00aRCRD.htm

Cost Methods: Under U.S. GAAP, the first in, first out (FIFO), last in, first out (LIFO) and weighted average costing methods are permissible. IFRS permits the use of FIFO and weighted average but does not allow the use of LIFO. This requirement constitutes a major challenge for retailers due to the potential tax implications resulting from the application of a valuation method other than LIFO. Many retailers use the Retail Inventory Method (RIM). IAS 2 permits the use of RIM" if the results approximate cost.: Additionally, IAS 2 requires that the RIM cost amounts be regularly reviewed to consider whether the results approximate cost. Therefore, retailers under RIM may need to develop and implement processes that permit them to make a regular review to determine whether the RIM amount continues to approximate actual cost. Another inventory consideration is that, under IFRS, inventory that is similar in nature must be accounted for using the same costing methodology.

Valuation and Reserves: Under U.S. GAAP, inventory generally is stated at the lower of cost or market. Market is defined as current replacement cost, an amount not greater than the net realizablc value nor less than the net realizable value less a normal profit margin. IFRS requires inventory to be started at the lower of cost or net realizable value. Net realizable value is the estimated selling price less the estimated cost of completion and sale. When inventory cost exceeds net realizable value of market, the inventory write down is recorded currently in profit or loss under IFRS and U.S. GAAP. However additional differences arise, similar to the accounting for property, plant and equipment, due to the fact that IFRS requires the reversal of inventory write down in subsequent periods if the value is recovered. Since, under this concept, no new cost basis is established with an inventory write down, this is an area that needs to be reviewed regularly and may require increased attention in the development of processes and systems during a conversion due to its systematic implications.

Allowances from Suppliers (IAS 2 and IAS 18): Allowances received from suppliers take different forms, including volume based incentives, scan promotions, price discounts (including for early payment), cooperative advertising, slotting and other programs. U.S. GAAP contains a presumption that any cash consideration received by a customer, including a reseller, from a vendor is a reduction of the cost of the vendor's product and is therefore, there must be clear evidence that the payment is for assets or services delivered to the vendor or a reimbursement of costs incurred by the customer to sell the vendor's products. Retailers may receive consideration from suppliers as a reimbursement of costs incurred. This consideration may be in the form of cash payments or rebates. Since IFRS has no prescriptive guidance and does not contain a 'rebuttable' presumption that the cash consideration is a reduction of the product cost, the transaction may need to be evaluated to determine if it is:

- Consideration received for assets or services delivered to the supplier, which should be recognized as revenue by the retailer if it relates to goods or services sold or delivered in the course of the ordinary activities or presented as other income if the activities are incidental to the retailer's main operations.
- Consideration that is reimbursement of costs incurred by an entity, which should be presented as a reduction of that cost.
- Consideration that represents a reduction in the prices of the manufacturer's product or services (trade discounts, volume rebates and other similar items) which should be presented as a reduction of the entity's inventory and therefore a reduction of cost of sales when the product is sold.

(b) Property, Plant and Equipment (IAS 16)

Component Approach: A component approach for depreciation of property, plant and equipment is permitted but not required under U.S. GAAP. IFRS has a requirement to segregate assets into individual components for determining appropriate useful lives and depreciation methods. IFRS also requires that the depreciation method selected be the one that most closely reflects the expected pattern of consumption of the asset. This may or may not be a significant issue depending on the level of detail that a company has historically used to identify individual asset.

Revaluation: U.S. GAAP does not allow for revaluation of PP&E to fair value, whereas IFRS allows as a policy election either a cost or revaluation model for each class of asset. To the extent a surplus from revaluation is recognized on an asset that was previously in a deficit position, the surplus would be recognized as a recovery in profit or loss to the extent of the previously recognized deficit.

(c) Intangible Assets (IAS 38)

Many retailers have been investing in new IT enabling technologies such as ERP systems, point of sale systems, logistics, and warehouse inventory management systems and e-commerce technologies to improve operation efficiency and customer experience while reducing costs. These internal use systems and software may represent a significant asset for a retailer.

Internal Use Software: U.S. GAAP includes specific guidance on the capitalization of internal use software. Under IFRS, there are no special requirements for the capitalization of internal use software and the costs are accounted for under the general principles of internally generated intangibles assets.

Useful Life Selection for Intangibles Assets: Under U.S. GAAP and IFRS, an intangible asset is either a finite lived or indefinite live asset, although the exact provisions of the standards differ in certain respects. For Finite lived intangible assets, the amortization method acceptable under U.S. GAAP and IFRS are generally consistent. Under both U.S. GAAP and IFRS, if the pattern of consumption of the economic benefits of the asset cannot be reliably determined, the straight line method is used. Under IFRS, the amortization method is reviewed at least at each annual reporting date while under U.S. GAAP, the amortization method is reviewed only when changes in events or circumstances indicate that the current estimate requires revision.

(d) Impairments (IAS 36)

Many retail companies have grown through acquisitions resulting in significant amounts of recognized goodwill and intangible assets. Due to the ever changing competitive landscape and the general economic environment, these assets can become impaired. Also, distribution centers, which are critical to success in the industry and can be a significant portion of a company's assets, can also become impaired.

Goodwill: Under both U.S. GAAP and IFRS, goodwill is not amortized and is subject to impairment tests annually or more frequently if indicators are present. Impairment charges under IFRS may occur earlier than under U.S. GAAP mainly for the following reasons:

- Impairment tests under U.S. GAAP are performed at the reporting unit (RU) level, while under IFRS, these tests are often performed at the cash generating unit level, which is the lowest level of assets that generates cash inflows from continuing use that are largely of the cash inflows of other assets and for which goodwill is monitored by management.
- In contrast to the two step impairment testing method required under U.S. GAAP, IFRS prescribes a one step impairment test, requiring loss recognition if the CGU's recoverable amount is less than its carrying amount. The recoverable amount equals the higher of the value in use (discounted entity specific future cash flows) or the fair value less costs to sell. Indefinite lived intangibles, long lived assets and finite lived intangibles: Under both U.S. GAAP and IFRS, indefinitelived intangibles are not amortized and are subject to impairment testing annually or more frequently if an indicator of impairment is identified.

Reversal of impairments: Under U.S. GAAP, the subsequent reversal of previously recognized impairment losses is prohibited. Under IFRS, reversal is required for identifiable assets (recovery is prohibited for goodwill) if circumstances leading to the impairment change in subsequent periods. The amount of the recovery is limited to what the carrying amount of the asset would have been had the impairment not been recognized.

(e) Leases (IAS 17)

Negotiating and securing lease arrangements for various facilities and equipment can be a significant business process of Retail companies.

Lease Classification: Unlike U.S. GAAP, IFRS does not contain bright lines that are used to classify a lease, but rather, provides indicators for determining the lease classification. Primary indicators assessed to determine whether substantially all of the risks and rewards are transferred include:

- The lease transfers ownership of the asset to the lessee by the end of the lease term.
- The lease contains a bargain purchase option.
- The lease term is for the major part of the economic life of the asset.
- The present value of the minimum lease payments amounts to at least substantially all of the fair value of the leased asset at the inception of the lease.
- The leased asset is of such a specialized nature that only the lessee can use it without major modifications.

Secondary Indicators are:

- The lessee would bear the lessor's losses associated with the cancellation of the lease by the lessee;
- Gains or losses from the fluctuation in the fair value of the residual accrue to the lessee;
- The lease contains a bargain renewal option.

(f) Defined Benefits Plans (IAS 19)

Many retail companies maintain defined benefit pension and or postretirement plans this is often a consequence of employing union workers and they may sponsor defined benefit plans. There can be significant differences between U.S. GAAP and IFRS in this area. Some of the differences are:

Actuarial Gains and Losses: Both U.S. GAAP and IFRS allow actuarial gains and losses on defined benefit plans to be recognized either using the corridor approach or immediately in current period cost. However IFRS also allows a third election, which is recognizing the gains and losses directly in other comprehensive income. A first time adopter of IFRS may elect to apply an exemption to recognize all cumulative actuarial gains and losses at the date of transition to IFRS as on adjustment to opening retained earnings. This option is available even if the entity will apply the corridor approach thereafter.

Plan Assets: The amount of prepaid pension cost under IFRS is limited based on a calculation of the sum of the present value of contribution reductions or refunds, unrecognized actuarial losses and unrecognized past service costs. There is detailed guidance on the application of the asset ceiling test and the minimum funding requirement liability in IFRIC 14, IAS 19.

Under IAS 19, Plan Assets are Either

- Assets held by a fund that is legally separate from the reporting entity and exists solely to pay or fund employee benefits and are not available to the reporting entity's creditors even in bankruptcy.
- Covered by qualifying insurance policies issued by an insurer that is not a related party of the reporting entity if the proceeds of the policy can be used only to pay or fund employee benefits under the plan and are not available to the reporting entity's own creditors, even in bankruptcy.

Balance Sheet Presentation: Under U.S. GAAP, the funded status of each individual plan (differences between the fair value of plan assets and the defined benefit obligation) is recognized as an asset if the plan is overfunded or as a liability if the plan is underfunded.

By contrast, under IFRS, a plan liability is recognized for the present value of the defined obligation, less the fair value of the plan assets, less unrecognized past service cost, and less (plus) unrecognized actuarial losses (gains). If the balance sheet amount is a net asset, then the amount recognized is the lower of the net asset amount and the lower of the net asset amount and the asset ceiling as determined by the guidance in IAS 19 and IFRIC 14.

Post-employment Benefits: Under IFRS, long term post employment benefits are accounted for in accordance with IAS 19. This is in contrast to U.S. GAAP, which makes a distinction between post employment benefits (after employment) and post retirement benefits (during retirement). The impact of a single standard of accounting for all post employment benefits under IFRS can be illustrated by the accounting for termination benefits. Under IFRS, a liability is not recognized until the company has issued a formal plan in sufficient detail along with a demonstrated commitment to the plan without a realistic possibility of withdrawal.

IFRS Impact on the Telecom, Tech and Media Firms

International Financial Reporting Standards (IFRS) will have a key impact on all convergence firms in the telecom, media and technology (TCE) sectors in myriad ways.

Whenever any component of a fixed asset will get replaced, its cost will be capitalized and the old components net written-down value will be removed from the fixed assets block. This will be a significant change for telecom firms, which are quite capital intensive. Further, for telecom base terminal stations and tower sites, the costs for site restoration would need to be factored upfront and included in the cost of the asset components. The major challenge here would be that many times it may not be evident from the contract whether an obligation exists or not. In IFRS, a provision would have to be made based on constructive obligation rather than legal obligation, so in all probability, such costs would need to be estimated and provided at the inception period of the terminal station or base site. For telecom firms, it will be critical to evaluate whether provision/receipt of infrastructure services constitutes or contains a lease arrangement under IFRIC-4 on Determining whether an Arrangement contains a Lease, particularly since it involves use of specific assets with a right to control the use of the asset.

Under Indian GAAP, such arrangements are considered as those for providing services and not a leasing activity. Technology firms may also have such arrangements under outsourcing contracts, data storage or network facility use arrangements, where IFRIC-4 will need to be evaluated for applicability.

Telecom companies provide package offers comprising handset, prepaid minutes, messages, discounts, special offers and other incentives. Technology firms also enter into lump sum contracts for sale of licences, implementation fees, warranty, maintenance and free upgrade services over a period of time. Media firms often bundle and market space across various products, programmes or channels and publications/portals. Under IFRS, a key issue will be to determine whether the various components of a transaction can be separated from an obligation performance standpoint and commercial perspective. In such cases, bundled contracts and multiple offerings under a package will require fair valuation of different components and revenues would be recognized accordingly. Indian GAAP does not provide any specific guidance on this and hence, inconsistent practices are presently being followed by various firms.

Under IFRS-2 on 'Share-based Payment', share-based payments also cover non-employees. If certain non-employee obligations are settled through employee stock options (Esops), IFRS will require fair value accounting for such options and cost differential between grant price and fair value will have to be recognized, either as a reduction of revenue or operating expense. Moreover, subsidiaries will need to account for Esop costs for options granted to its employees by the parent company with corresponding impact in capital contribution by the parent as per the requirement of IFRIC-11 on IFRS 2—Group and Treasury Share Transactions. This is not required under Indian GAAP. Another key aspect is that Indian GAAP allows intrinsic method of accounting. Here the Esop cost is generally lower since it only takes into account the value of the option as at the date of its grant and does not capture the likely accretion in fair value over the entire vesting period. Share based payment costs are expected to increase on application of IFRS. IFRS entails discounting of receivables and payables to their current values using expected interest rates. In telecom firms, this concept of time value of money will have impact on the amounts recorded for long-term security deposits, payables falling due after a year and revenues earned in advance for long-term subscription arrangements.

In summary, convergence to IFRS for the new-age convergence firms is not going to be a cakewalk and will need significant preparation well in advance, so that they are ready for the IFRS Goes Live event effective 1 April 2010.

IFRS Impact on the Extractive Sector (Oil and Gas Sector)

The implementation of standards prescribed by the transition from Canadian GAAP to IFRS will require some of the most complex judgements that the oil and gas industry has had to face relative to financial accounting. The industry demands large upfront investments and most often, there is great uncertainty in the long-term prospects of those investments. More than 70 countries have mandated the use of IFRS and Canadian public enterprises are required to make the transition as of 1 January 2011.

Price water house Coopers. (PWC), has worked with companies around the globe assisting them with their adoption of IFRS, indicates that it may take from two to five years to fully convert and implement the proposed new standards. IFRS will require that businesses in the oil and gas sector implement changes in communication with investors, analysts and all other stakeholders. One of the first considerations that oil and gas companies need to engage is with the determination of which differences have application on their particular organization. The AcSB has attempted to assist companies in addressing this issue by establishing an IFRS implementation schedule that will continue to impact publicly accountable entities, as those responsible for setting and establishing standards across the globe continue to harmonize their frameworks. However, companies will have to be as responsive to emerging changes as they are with the initial transition and implementation, particularly when a change has a direct effect on their particular organization.

Accounting: Many global integrated oil and gas companies use the "successful efforts" method of accounting, which involves capitalizing the costs to locate, acquire and develop reserves on a field by field basis. Under this method of accounting, when a commercially viable reserve is discovered, capitalized costs may be allocated to the discovery. If such a discovery is not achieved, the expenditure is considered an expense. Geological and geophysical costs are also generally expensed. IFRS limits this type of accounting to exploration and evaluation activities only. All costs incurred for all other activities must be accounted for on a successful efforts type basis.

The IASB has commenced a project to review the accounting practices and models applied globally in the oil and gas industry. Until this project is complete, IFRS 6 is the interim standard. It allows public entities to continue with their accounting practices relative to exploration and evaluation.

Accounting for Impairment: The implementation of IFRS to allocate costs at field level becomes particularly complex for the issue of impairment. IFRS rules regarding impairment require companies to assess historical data for assets in impairment. That can be a problem for companies in this industry since it is often times difficult to extract such data.

IFRS requires that impairment tests be performed at the field level once an impairment indicator has been identified. At the field level, the smallest groups of assets that are responsible to generate cash flow independent of other assets or asset groups are known as an individual cash generating unit (CGU).

IFRS Impact on the Microfinance Sector

The Microfinance Reporting Standards Initiative is gaining momentum...with lots of new activity, including a standards adoption process adapted from the International Accounting Standards Board (IASB).

Given that MFIs worldwide do not uniformly follow standards and are only beginning to use new tools like IFRS for financial reporting, the discussion raised more questions than answers. The initiative will continue to facilitate conversation and education so that sector stakeholders may access information on the key issues in reporting under IFRS. More data is also needed—both on the differences between national accounting standards and IFRS, as well as the experience of MFIs that have used both.

Nevertheless, three clear themes emerged from the discussion:

1. Implementation of IFRS is a capacity-building challenge–for MFIs, local audit firms, investors and stakeholders generally.
2. Insufficient data exists on the differences between national accounting standards and IFRS and available information is not widely circulated or accessed.
3. As the microfinance industry matures, new financial reporting ratios will be needed.

To have a better depth on these points the following details have been given.

1. IFRS as a Capacity-building Challenge

Implementing IFRS for MFI financial reporting appears to challenge the capacity of the entire spectrum of stakeholders in microfinance, from central banks to MFI boards of directors to accounting and auditing professionals to international PVOs and networks to MFI staff.

Muhammad Junaid of the United Nations Capital Development Fund (UNCDF) suggested IFRS should be addressed at three levels: policy, regulation, and training and capacity building. First, governments and central banks must be encouraged to adapt IFRS into national accounting standards. Such an effort requires a government champion that can coordinate a national effort with other major stakeholders. At the level of regulation, there are two capacity issues. "Central banks lack the capacity (and in most cases, the willingness, to regulate the microfinance industry," observed Junaid. Even if IFRS was required for reporting to regulatory authorities, as several participants in the discussion suggested, Junaid pointed out that the majority of MFIs in many countries lack the capacity to prepare and submit professionally prepared accounting statements complying with national or international standards. No amount of regulation can make up for the lack of capacity within MFIs." Junaid concluded that, "Training and capacity building of the industry and at the organizational level are the most important [element needed] to introduce effective reporting standards." Junaid explained that mobilizing support from a wide range of stakeholders is the key to success. "Effective stakeholder participation in the policymaking process is critical," he explained, Financial sector associations, accounting, and auditing professional bodies and donors can play a significant role in the adaptation, translation, and dissemination of relevant reporting standards."

In addition to capacity building of regulatory authorities and the accounting profession, IFRS also requires Board members with new skills. Disclosures are significantly more detailed for external audits [under IFRS], which increases the costs of the audits, and [makes] additional demands on board members to understand them. IFRS implementation itself depends on a motivated member of the board: "From working with a number of MFIs, the accounting policies being proposed and implemented are often a matter of training and experience of the accountant or member of the Board that pushes this [idea], which can be a key limitation."

Depending on the country, MFIs may initially adopt IFRS or transition to IFRS from the national accounting standards that previously governed their financial reporting.

2. Insufficient Data Exists on the Differences between National Accounting Standards and IFRS

Available information is not widely circulated or accessed. A number of participants pointed out that the differences between national standards and IFRS were not yet well understood. The same applies to differences between IFRS and GAAP, the application of which also vary by country.

The new demands that IFRS makes on MFI record-keeping and accounting practices, including:

- tracking of additional information, such as loan interest accruals, exchange rates and maturity gaps of assets and liabilities;
- recognition of loan commissions and fees over the life of a loan instead of at the time of receipt far more detailed disclosure in external audits;
- methods of measuring the impairments of assets, particularly loans receivables.

In countries that have not yet elaborated national accounting standards, IFRS may be adopted by straightaway by the banking and/or microfinance regulatory authority. In other countries, MFIs may use different standards when preparing financial reporting for different stakeholders: national standards for regulatory authorities and IFRS for international donors and investors.

3. As the Microfinance Industry Matures, New Financial Reporting Ratios may be Needed

Several participants agreed that new MFI reporting ratios would be needed as the industry continues to mature, including deposit concentration and capital adequacy ratios in regulated institutions. In addition, Nancy Sommer of responsibility, a social investment firm, noted that an open currency position ratio (% of equity plus subordinated-debt) and refinancing and/or restructuring ratios were becoming more useful.

The management information system (MIS) may have to be altered to track new data, such as the capacity to accrue interest on outstanding loans, track exchange rates and maturity gaps, and possibly to recognize commissions and fees over the life of the associated loans; support from knowledgeable Board members will be needed for successful implementation; certain flexibility, such as the ability to renegotiate payment schedules, might be lost because of the confusion over how to categorize renegotiated loans under IFRS.

Impact of IFRS on the Public Sector

The transition to IFRS may be more significant for some public sector bodies than others. The most significant issues for public sector bodies are expected to include the accounting for PFI schemes and similar arrangements, the treatment of derivatives embedded within other contracts and lease accounting. A summary of the key issues is shown in the following table.

TOPIC AREA	IMPLICATIONS UNDER IFRS
PFI	• Potentially moving schemes on balance sheet using principles of 'control' rather than 'risk' and 'reward'.
Leases	• Need to separately account for leases of land and buildings.
	• Land leases are normally operating leases.
	• Experience shows that the detailed review of leases between operating and finance leases is time consuming.
	• Other contracts with 'lease type' features need to be identified.
Segment reporting	• Segment must correspond with internal reporting. • Reconciliation to reported financial information.
Financial instrument/ embedded derivatives	• Very complicated standards. • Cover a large part of the balance sheet. • New and extensive disclosures. • Separate accounting for derivatives (and embedded derivatives).
Staff benefits (leave	• Stricter requirements to include accruals for staff benefits such as accrued leave.
Increased disclosures	• IFRS requires increased disclosures in the financial statements, driving up the length of financial statements and the amount of time required to collect the supporting data.

Source: From Price water house Coopers Access IFRS website at: www.ifrs.co.uk/index.html

Conclusion

With rapid liberalization process experienced in India over the past decade, there is now a huge presence of multinational enterprises in the country. Furthermore, Indian companies are also investing in foreign markets. This has generated an interest in Indian GAAPs by all concerned. In this context, the role of Indian accounting standards, which are becoming closure to IFRSs, has assumed a greater significance from the point of view of global financial reporting.

Indian companies using the Indian accounting standards are experiencing fewer difficulties accessing international financial markets, are Indian accounting standards are becoming closer to the IFRSs. Indian standards are expected to converge even further in thee future, especially after the challenges mentioned in study are addressed over the next few years.

These IFRS standards when followed by different sectors in India will have different impact in all the sectors. When coming to the revenue recognition Technology, Media, Real estate and infrastructure and Telecom industry will high impact where as sectors like Pharmaceutical, Retail and Extractive sector industries will have moderate impact. Moving to the major overhauling expenses Pharmaceutical, Real Estate and Infrastructure and Extractive sector industries will have high impact where as Retail and Telecom sector industries will have moderate impact, comparatively Technology and Media will have lower impact. Coming to the revaluation of PPE Pharmaceutical, Real Estate and Infrastructure and Extractive sector industries have higher impact compared to Retail who will have moderate impact and Technology, Media and Telecom sector who will have lower impact. Moving to the Provisions (Discounting) Real Estate and Infrastructure and Extractive sector industries will have higher impact compared to Pharmaceutical and Telecom industries that have moderate impact and Technology, Retail and Media who have lower impact. Thus, more or less all will be affected either highly or moderately or lowly by the impact of IFRS when it is going to converge with the Indian GAAP.

The Convergence with IFRS Entails Benefit to the Following:

- *The Investors;* The investor will be benefited in as the way accounting information made available to them will be more reliable, relevant, timely and most importantly the information will be comparable across different legal framework. It will develop better understanding and confidence among the investors.
- *The Professional:* The professional, both in practice and in employment will get benefits as they will be able to provide their services in various part of the world, as few years after everybody will follow the same reporting standards.
- *The Corporate World:* The Indian corporate reputation and relationship with international finance community will elevate because of achievement of higher level of consistency between reporting structure and requirements; better access to international markets; improving confidence among the international investors. The international comparability will also get improve strengthening the industrial and capital markets in the country.

REFERENCES

1. Sharma, Bhavesh , "IFRS—Challenges and Needs for India INC", http://www.indianmba.com/ Articles_on_Management/AOM49/aom49.html.
2. Grimley .GVA, "IFRS Implication to Public Sector Property Assets", http://www.gvagrimley.co.uk/Documents/IFRS % 20 Implications % 20 to % 20 Public % 20 Sector % 20 Property % 20 Assets.pdf.
3. Souza.D.Dolphy (2010), "IFRS Impact on Retail Sector", http://www.thehindubusinessline.com/mentor/2010/03/29/stories/2010032950351100.ht.
4. Venkataraman.N(2010), "IFRS Impact on Few Key Sectors", http://www.thehindu.com/business/article455320.ece.
5. Agarwal.N (2009), "Convergence to IFRS: Impact to IT Sector" , http://www.expresscomputeronline.com/20090601/management03.shtml.
6. Deloitte (2009), "Summary of IFRS Developments that May Impact the Real Estate Sector", http://www.deloitte.com/view/en_LU/lu/industries/real-estate/article/931c6d4de4e76210 Vgn VCM 100000 ba 42 f00a RCRD.htm.

7. KPMG, "Implication of IFRS for Retail Sector", https://www.in.kpmg.com/securedata/ifrs_Institute/Files/Implications_of_IFRS_for_the_Retail_Sector.pdf.
8. KPMG, "IFRS Convergence: Challenges and Implementation Approaches for Banks in India", https://www.in.kpmg.com/securedata /ifrs_Institute/Files/IFRS Convergence for the India bankingsector.pdf.
9. Price Water Coopers, "International Financial Reporting Standards – Issues and Solutions for Pharmaceutical and Life Science Industries, Vol. III, http://www.pwc.com/gx/en/pharma-life-sciences/international-financial-reporting-standards-ifrs-issues-solutions-for-pharmaceutical-life-sciences.jhtml.
10. KC0204 Wong Report (2004), "Challenges and Success in Implementing International Standards: Achieving Convergence to IFRS and ISAs", web.ifac.org/.../6/challenges-and-successes.../challenges-and-successes-in.pdf.
11. Price Water Coopers , "Putting IFRS in Motion —The Impact of Financial Reporting Standards (IFRS) on the Canadian Real Estate Sector", http:/www.pwc.com/en_CA/ca/ifrs/publications/ifrs-realestate-0808-en.pdf.
12. Corporate Sector Review (2005), "Selling the Standards", KPMG, "IFRS and Pharmaceutical Companies", https://www.in.kpmg.com/securedata/ifrs_Institute/Files/IFRSforPharma.pdf .
13. The Seep Network, USAID from the American People, "New Development in MFI Reporting Standards", http://www.seepnetwork.org/Resources/6172_file_MF_Standards_ Committee_ concept_note _logo_up_11.09.08_ONLINE.pdf.

Index

D

E

F

G

H

J

– × – × –